Kitchen Makeover page 09

Cooking Tips page 16

JumpStart page 29

Breakfast page 59

Salads and Vegetables page 69

Soups page 95

Light Meals page 105

Main Meals page 119

Spreads and Dips page 145

Desserts page 155

GUIDELINES FOR *Optimal Eating*

It is our joy to share with you some of our favorite recipes to inspire you! Each of the recipes in the *Eat More* cookbook emphasizes the use of nurturing whole plant foods. These guidelines for optimal eating help you achieve and maintain good health.

PER DAY RECOMMENDATIONS

Fiber > 40 grams
Water 8 glasses
Cholesterol < 50 milligrams
Fats & Oils < 40 grams
Sodium < 1800 milligrams or *Salt* < 5 grams
Refined Sugars* < 40 grams

*Includes cane sugar, honey, maple syrup, molasses and other concentrated sweeteners.

Introduction

The philosophy of this book is based on the simple joys and inherent goodness of eating wholesome, delicious foods. It celebrates that the act of preparing, sharing and enjoying combinations of nature's whole plant foods with family and friends can nourish our body, mind, heart and spirit. These recipes collectively affirm that "foods as grown" not only provide optimal nourishment but also proactively prevent, manage and even reverse many lifestyle diseases, enhancing our quality and length of life! We invite you to "eat more" . . . as part of a full and abundant life.

Cathy McDonald
Board Director, Lifestyle Medicine Institute, LLC
Accredited Practicing Dietitian

The Optimal Diet

EAT LESS ⌄

› **Fats and oils:** Avoid fatty meats. Strictly limit cooking and salad oils, sauces, dressings, shortening, margarine and butter. Use nuts sparingly. Avoid frying (sauté with some water in non-stick pan). Especially avoid saturated fat and trans fats (for example, cookies, crackers and bakery products).

› **Sugars:** Limit sugar, honey, molasses, syrups, pies, cakes, pastries, candies, chocolates, cookies, soda/soft drinks, and sugar-rich desserts like pudding and ice cream. Use these foods sparingly and/or for special occasions only.

› **Foods containing cholesterol:** Avoid meat, sausages, eggs and liver. If consuming dairy, limit intake and ensure labeled non-fat or low-fat. If consuming fish and poultry, eat sparingly.

› **Salt:** Use minimal salt during cooking. Strictly limit highly salted products like cured meats, crackers, soy sauce, salted popcorn, salted nuts, snacks, chips, pretzels and garlic salt.

› **Alcohol and Caffeine:** Avoid alcohol in all forms. Avoid or gradually eliminate caffeinated beverages, such as coffee, black tea, caffeinated energy drinks and soda/soft drinks.

EAT MORE ⌃

› **Whole grains:** Freely use brown rice, millet, barley, corn, wheat, rye, oats, quinoa and amaranth. Also eat freely a variety of whole grain products, such as breads, pastas, breakfast cereal and tortillas.

› **Legumes:** Freely use all kinds of legumes. Enjoy peas, lentils, garbanzos/chickpeas and beans of every kind.

› **Fruits and vegetables:** Eat several fresh, whole fruits every day. Limit fruits canned in syrup and fiber-poor fruit juices. Eat a variety of vegetables daily (without high-fat toppings). Enjoy fresh salads with low-calorie, low-sodium dressings.

› **Water:** Drink eight glasses of water a day. Vary the routine with a twist of lemon or use herbal teas.

› **Wholesome breakfasts:** Enjoy hot multigrain cereals, fresh fruit, whole grain breakfast cereals and whole grain toast. Make breakfast a big deal.

Energy Density of Foods

Choosing plant-based whole foods takes the stress out of weight loss. These foods are packed with nutrients (nutrient dense) but most have relatively low calories, sodium and saturated fat. Choosing whole foods is also an easy way to increase your fiber intake in some of your favorite meals.

EAT LESS

EAT MORE

VERSUS

CARROT CAKE WITH ICING
1 slice, 5.3 ounces (150 grams) **503 calories (2103 kJ)**

16 CARROTS
3.5 pounds (1570 grams) **503 calories (2103 kJ)**

IN SUMMARY: Freely eat a wide variety of "foods as grown" simply prepared with sparing use of fats and oils, sugars and salt. Use refined products and animal products only on special occasions. Enjoy food with friends and family and create a lifetime of memories. Choose life!

"Nothing will benefit human health and increase the chances for survival of life on earth as much as the evolution to a vegetarian diet."

[Albert Einstein]

Kitchen Makeover

We know how busy life can be. Having a well organized kitchen, fridge, freezer and pantry is the first step to making healthier food choices. It can also help you save time and money. Create a safe food environment by keeping the following foods readily available:

GRAINS (choose mostly whole grains) Best stored in airtight containers.

- Whole Grain Pasta
- Whole Grain Wheat
- Bulgur Wheat
- Shredded Wheat

- Couscous
- Rolled Oats
- Quick-cooking Oats
- Pearl Barley

- Quinoa (GF)
- Buckwheat (GF)
- Popcorn Kernels (plain) (GF)
- 100% Whole Wheat Flour

- Millet (GF)
- Amaranth (GF)
- Cornmeal/Polenta (GF)
- Brown Rice (GF)

PANTRY BASICS

- Canned Tomatoes (no-added-salt)
- Tomato Paste (no-added-salt)
- Sundried Tomatoes (no oil)
- Soy Sauce (low-sodium)
- Apple Sauce (unsweetened)

- Dried Herbs and Spices
- Soy or Other Non-dairy Milk fortified with calcium and B12
- Nutritional Yeast Flakes
- Light Coconut Milk (optional)
- Chicken-like Flavoring (low-sodium)

- Whole Grain Crackers
- Rice Cakes
- Puffed Wheat
- Puffed Rice or Corn
- Whole Grain Breakfast Cereals

(GF) - Gluten Free

FRESH PRODUCE
- Seasonal Fruit—including berries, bananas, stone fruit and citrus fruit such as oranges, lemons and limes.
- Seasonal Vegetables—including green leafy vegetables and staples such as potatoes, onions, peas, beans, corn and carrots.
- Herbs and Spices—try growing your own.

BAKING ESSENTIALS
- Baking Powder
- Arrowroot Powder
- Corn Starch/Cornflour
- Honey
- Egg Replacer
- Vegetable Oil
- Non-stick Cooking Spray
- Agar Agar Powder

FROZEN
- Fruit—such as berries and peaches.
- Vegetables—minimally processed without salt or fat, not French fries.

MEAT ALTERNATIVES
- Tofu
- Tempeh
- Beans, Lentils and Nuts

NUT BUTTERS
- Almond
- Peanut
- Tahini

LEGUMES (beans, lentils and split peas) Best stored in airtight containers.

DRY

- Lentils (red/green/brown)
- White Beans
- Split Peas
- Black Beans
- Pinto Beans

CANNED (low-sodium)

- Kidney Beans
- Garbanzos/Chickpeas
- Black Eyed Peas
- Brown Lentils
- Cannellini or Lima/Butter Beans
- Pinto Beans
- Black Beans
- Navy/Great Northern Beans

NUTS AND SEEDS

Use nuts and seeds sparingly, preferably in their natural condition, raw and unsalted. While they contain many vitamins and minerals, they are also high in calories. If not used quickly, nuts and seeds are best stored in the fridge or freezer.

- Almonds
- Walnuts
- Sesame Seeds
- Pine Nuts
- Cashews
- Hazelnuts
- Coconut (unsweetened)
- Brazil Nuts
- Peanuts
- Flax Seeds
- Chia Seeds
- Pumpkin Seeds
- Pecans
- Sunflower Seeds

SWEETENERS

Use sweeteners carefully as nearly all are high calorie.

- Molasses
- Stevia Leaf Powder
- Maple Syrup
- Pitted Dates, Figs or Prunes
- Honey
- Agave Nectar

OILS AND FATS

Use only minimal amounts and only from plant sources. Store oil in a cool dark area.

When stocking up on pantry basics, remind yourself to try out new foods on a regular basis. Variety is the spice of life!

Herbs and Spices
Flavor with herbs and spices

Herbs and spices are a great way to add flavor and taste to dishes.

Fresh herbs can be stored in the refrigerator crisper for as long as six days. Loosely wrap herbs in paper towel and place them in a plastic zip-type/long-life bag. You can also chop them and keep in the fridge for a few days in airtight containers lined with paper towel.

Only some herbs will freeze well, such as basil, chives and tarragon. Wrap in foil or seal in a plastic bag or container.

Herbs
Some common herbs and their uses

› **Basil:** Has a rich peppery flavor and powerful aroma. This herb is particularly good when served with tomatoes, and is often used in Italian and Mediterranean dishes.

› **Chives:** A bright green herb with an onion flavor. Best served on potato salads, baked potatoes and some soups or use in sandwich spreads and dips. Provides a good flavor contrast for bland dishes.

› **Cilantro/Coriander:** A strong-flavored herb that appears similar to flat-leaf parsley. It is often used with chili powder, garlic, ginger and spring onions in Thai dishes, Mexican cuisine, stir-fries and salsas.

› **Dill:** A delicately flavored herb that complements boiled potatoes. Can also be used in sauces, dips and salad dressings.

› **Fennel Leaves:** Similar to dill but a stronger flavor.

› **Marjoram/Oregano:** These two herbs are different varieties of the same plant. Often used in Mediterranean tomato-based dishes.

› **Mint:** A fresh-flavored herb, often used in salads in the Middle East. Mint is a great addition to soups or salsas.

› **Parsley:** Two types of parsley can be used in cooking— curly and flat. Both can be used in soups, salads and with beans or lentils.

› **Rosemary:** This herb has a very strong flavor. It complements potatoes and baked vegetable dishes.

› **Sage:** A strong-flavored herb that goes well with onions. Use in soups, stuffing, pasta sauces, and bean or lentil stews.

› **Tarragon:** Fresh tarragon has a sweet and spicy flavor, and complements many vegetables. It is particularly nice with potatoes.

› **Thyme:** Best used in bean or lentil stews or soups with tomatoes.

Spices

Some common spices and their uses

› **Chili Powder:** Has a fiery flavor and goes well with beans and vegetables. It can be used in soup and salads, as well as legume and vegetable dishes.

› **Cinnamon:** Add a sprinkle of ground cinnamon to rolled oats or muesli and fruit desserts. Whole cinnamon sticks can also be added to legume and vegetable curry dishes.

› **Cloves:** Use whole or ground in soup or vegetables. Also goes well with fruit.

› **Cumin:** This spice is a popular flavor in many cuisines. It is nearly always used in curry powder.

› **Curry Powder:** Curry powder is usually a combination of many types of spices, including turmeric, cumin, cilantro/coriander, cardamom, chili and curry leaves. Curry powder gives extra flavor to vegetable, bean or lentil soups, stews and curries.

› **Fennel Seed:** These seeds have a slight anise seed flavor. They can be used in curries, soups and stews or baked into bread.

› **Garam Masala:** A spice blend that usually contains cumin, cloves, cinnamon, cardamom and nutmeg. For a powerful flavor boost, add the mixture in the last minutes of cooking.

› **Ginger, fresh:** Look for firm, shiny ginger roots. Finely chop or grate ginger into dishes such as soups, salads, stews, stir-fries and curries. Goes well with onion and garlic.

› **Ginger, powdered:** Mostly used in sweet dishes with fruit, but also used in savory dishes along with curry or tomatoes.

› **Nutmeg:** If possible, buy whole and grate as needed. Great for flavoring soups, vegetables, breads and sweets. Try adding to a tomato-based pasta sauce.

› **Paprika:** Made from finely ground dried red bell pepper/capsicum. Use in soups, sauces, salads and dips or spreads.

› **Turmeric:** Commonly available in a powdered form. Adds a bright yellow color to foods.

TIP: Spices begin to lose flavor after prolonged storage. For the best flavor, store in airtight containers in a cool, dark place and use within three months.

Salt Substitute Seasoning Suggestions

Salt Substitute Seasoning 1

- 2 teaspoons ground oregano
- 5 teaspoons onion powder
- 2 teaspoons garlic powder
- 2 teaspoons ground paprika
- 2 teaspoons dried thyme
- ¼ teaspoon celery seed or celery salt

Mix all ingredients well and store in airtight container.

Salt Substitute Seasoning 2

- 1 tablespoon garlic powder
- 1 tablespoon onion powder
- 1 tablespoon dried basil
- 2 teaspoons dried oregano
- 2 teaspoons dried rosemary

Mix all ingredients well and store in airtight container.

Use your favorite herbs and spices to create your own salt substitute seasoning.

Use as little salt as possible for seven days and see how your taste changes.

Try using salt substitute seasonings to replace salt in these **Eat More** recipes to further reduce your sodium intake.

Cooking Tips
A handy guide to cooking with grains

Unless otherwise specified, bring liquid (water or broth) to a boil, stir in grain, reduce to low heat and simmer in covered pan.

GRAIN TYPE	GRAIN:LIQUID	COOKING TIME
Amaranth (GF)	1 cup: 3 cups	Simmer 25-30 minutes. Do not salt until thoroughly cooked.
Basmati Rice (brown) (GF)	1 cup: 2 cups	Simmer 40-45 minutes.
Basmati Rice (white) (GF)	1 cup: 1¾ cups	Simmer 20 minutes.
Brown Rice (short or long grain) (GF)	1 cup: 2 or 2½ cups	Simmer 45-60 minutes.
Bulgur Wheat	1 cup: 2½ cups	Simmer 25 minutes, fluff with fork, let sit for 10 minutes. Or boil the water, pour over bulgur wheat, cover and let sit for 1 hour.
Cornmeal/Polenta (GF)	1 cup: 4 cups	Bring 2½ cups water to a boil. Combine cornmeal with 1½ cups cold water and ½ teaspoon salt, then slowly add to boiling water; stir until boiling resumes. Reduce to low heat and cook covered 10 to 15 minutes, stirring occasionally.
Couscous (pronounced KOOS-koos)	1 cup: 1½ cups	Add couscous to boiling water. Remove from heat, stir, cover and let stand for 10 minutes. Fluff with fork.
Millet (GF)	1 cup: 2-2½ cups	Simmer 15 minutes, remove from heat, fluff, and let sit uncovered for 20 minutes.
Pearl Barley	1 cup: 4 cups	Simmer 60-70 minutes.
Wild and Brown Rice Mix (GF)	1 cup: 3 cups	Simmer 35 minutes or check instructions on package.
Quinoa (GF) (pronounced KEEN-wah)	1 cup: 2-3 cups	Rinse quinoa in a strainer, then add to pot along with water. Cover and bring to a boil for 10 minutes or until water is absorbed. Fluff with fork, and cover until time to serve.

(GF) - Gluten Free

Source: Colleen Patrick-Goudreau (2011), The 30 Day Vegan Challenge, Ballantine Books, page 52.

Quinoa

A nutritious, nutrient-dense seed that possesses many grain-like qualities. It is a great gluten-free option, comes in a variety of colors—white, red and black—and is bursting with antioxidants.

Cooking with beans and lentils

CROCK POT METHOD: Soaking is not required for this method, simply rinse beans/lentils thoroughly and place in crock pot with water (see table on page 19 for amount). Add ¼ teaspoon salt per 1 cup of dry beans/lentils, cover and cook on low for 8-12 hours. For faster cooking, use high setting for all or part of the cooking time. Lentils, split peas and small beans may take less time to cook.

PRESOAKING: Check beans and lentils for stones, rinse well then cover with plenty of water and soak using one of the methods below.

SOAKING METHODS	INSTRUCTIONS
Overnight soak	Let stand 12 hours or overnight.
Quick soak	Bring beans/lentils and water to a boil. Boil gently for 2 minutes. Turn off heat, cover and let stand for 1 hour.
Microwave soak	Combine legumes and water in microwave dish. Cover and microwave on high for 10-15 minutes. Let stand for 1 hour.

Source: Pulse Canada (2012), Winnipeg, Canada, <www.pulsecananda.com>.

FREEZING TIP: Cooked beans and lentils can be stored in the freezer for up to six months. Separate into serving sizes before freezing and place in individual freezer bags or small containers.

18 | Complete Health Improvement Program – **EAT MORE**

Stovetop cooking methods and times for beans and lentils

After soaking, drain water and rinse, place beans or lentils into a saucepan with water (check table below for quantity).
Bring to a boil, add ¼ to ½ teaspoon salt per cup of beans, reduce heat, cover and simmer until tender (see table below for times).
Note: information provided in the table is a guide only. It is the responsibility of the cook to ensure beans and lentils are cooked before use.

	Beans	Whole Peas	Split Peas	Whole Lentils	Split Lentils	Garbanzos /Chickpeas	Split Garbanzos /Chickpeas
Rinse	Yes	Yes	Yes	Yes	Yes	Yes	Yes
Soak	Yes	Yes	No	No	No	Yes	No
Amount of water for cooking per 1 cup (8 fl oz/250ml) legumes	2½-3 cups	2½-3 cups	2 cups	2½-3 cups	2 cups	2½-3 cups	2 cups
Cooking time	1-2+ hours	1-1½ hours	45 minutes	30-45 minutes	5-15 minutes	1½-2+ hours	½-1 hour
Yield from 1 cup (8 fl oz/250ml) legumes	2½ cups	2½ cups	2 cups	2½ cups	2 cups	2½ cups	2 cups

Source: Pulse Canada (2012), Winnipeg, Canada, <www.pulsecananda.com>.

Adapting popular recipes for plant-based eating

It's easy to make your favorite recipes plant-based. Simply replace dairy products with plant-based substitutes and use good meat replacements. Here are some ideas to get you started:

	ALTERNATIVES	BEST IN . . . (Choose low-fat, if available.)
Dairy Milk	**Soy Milk***	Soy milk has a distinct flavor and can be used as a direct replacement in most recipes.
	Almond Milk*	Almond milk can be used as a direct replacement in most recipes. Use the unsweetened variety, if available.
	Rice Milk*	Rice milk can be used in most recipes. Check the label first and choose the unsweetened variety, if available.
	Oat Milk*	Oat milk can be used as a direct milk replacement in most recipes.
	Coconut Milk	Coconut milk is great used in curries, Asian-style dishes, soups and smoothies. Choose 'lite' if available, as it is lower in saturated fat. Use sparingly.

*fortified with calcium and vitamin B12

	ALTERNATIVES	BEST IN ...	TIPS
Eggs	**Ground Flax Seed/Chia Seed** (GF)	Waffles, pancakes, bran muffins, breads, oatmeal cookies, sprinkle on breakfast cereal	Flax seeds and chia seeds are both a great source of omega 3. Use 1-2 tablespoons per day.
	Ripe Bananas (GF)	Breads, muffins, cakes, pancakes	Be sure to use baking powder or baking soda in your recipe as well, because bananas will not help it rise or become light and fluffy.
	Apple Sauce (unsweetened) (GF)	Cakes, quick breads, brownies	Apple sauce is best substituted in sweet dishes, as it has a sweet flavor.
	Soft/Silken Tofu	Waffles, pancakes, bran muffins, breads, oatmeal cookies	Useful for making creamy recipes, such as dips, puddings and pie fillings. This type of tofu is not recommended for stir-fries or broiling/grilling, as it is likely to fall apart.
	Firm Tofu	Patties, scramble and sandwich spread	Great for making scrambled tofu (see page 110), as it has a soft texture much like scrambled egg.
	Corn Starch/Corn Flour (GF)	Gravy, sauces, soups, stews, puddings	Great for thickening.
	Arrowroot Powder (GF)	Gravy, sauces, soups, stews, puddings	Dissolves well and is a great thickener.

(GF) - Gluten Free

	ALTERNATIVES	TIPS
Cheese	**Dairy Free Cheese Alternatives**	There are a wide variety of dairy-free cheese alternatives available today. Check your local supermarket or health-food shop for different options. Be sure to read the label, as some may contain casein. Choose options that are fortified with calcium and vitamin B12, and are minimally processed. Use sparingly.
	Cashew Cheese	This can be used in place of traditional cheese. It can be grated, sliced and melted. See recipe on page 153 to make your own. Use sparingly.
Sour Cream	**Sunflower Seed Cream**	To make sunflower seed cream, simply use the recipe for Cashew Cream on page 146 and substitute sunflower seeds for the cashews.

	ALTERNATIVES	TIPS
Cream	**Coconut Milk**	Has a distinct flavor, and can be used successfully in both savory and sweet dishes. Use sparingly.
	Sweet Cashew Cream	Can be used in place of cream in many recipes. See recipe on page 149 to make your own. Use sparingly.
	Other Sweet Nut Creams	Create your own sweet nut cream using the Sweet Cashew Cream recipe on page 149 and replace cashews with nuts of your choice. Try using sunflower seeds, macadamia nuts or almonds for extra variety. Use sparingly.

	ALTERNATIVES	TIPS
Yogurt	**Soy Yogurt**	There are a number of soy-based yogurts on the market today. Check your local supermarket or health food shop to see the range. Use sparingly.
	Coconut Yogurt	Coconut yogurt is another yogurt alternative, which is great especially if you have an allergy to soy. Use sparingly.

	ALTERNATIVES	TIPS
Margarine or Butter	**Avocado**	A great whole food replacement for margarine. Use on toast or sandwiches.
	Hummus	Can be purchased in the dip section of your local supermarket, or make your own, see page 152. Great on toast or sandwiches.

	ALTERNATIVES	TIPS
Mayonnaise	**Eggless Mayonnaise**	Check your local supermarket or health-food shop for eggless mayonnaise. Be sure to check the label first. Or make your own, see page 146. Use sparingly.

	ALTERNATIVES	TIPS
Meat	**Lentils, Beans, Nuts**	These are all great meat alternatives that can be used in a variety of different ways. Replace ground/minced meat with brown lentils in a lasagna or in pasta sauce, and replace meat with beans in a hearty stew.
	Extra-firm Tofu	Will not lose its shape. Marinate, BBQ, fry in a skillet/frypan, or under the broil/grill element. Great for using in stir-fries and curries.
	Tempeh	Tempeh has a slightly nutty flavor and firm chewy texture. To enhance the flavor, steam for 10 minutes before cooking. Broil/grill, fry, sauté, marinate or bake. Add to a stir-fry, crumble into pasta sauce, BBQ or grate and add to your favorite dish.

"If you want to be a winner in the losing game, you have to eat more!" [Dr Hans Diehl]

Eat More

Eat More: Quicker

These ratings will help you identify which recipes are quick and easy to prepare and those worth the time and effort for special occasions.

Our ratings help to convey: **Affordability and Simplicity • Convenience • Confidence**

Super Quick and Easy	Investing in good food	Worth the time and effort
Up to 6 ingredients	At least 6 ingredients	At least 6 ingredients
Up to 30 minutes total preparation and cooking time	30 to 45 minutes total preparation and cooking time	At least 45 minutes total preparation and cooking time
Up to 3 steps	3 or more steps	More than 3 steps, may include more complex cooking techniques

TIP: It is helpful to remember that some recipes will be quick to prepare, but may have more than 6 ingredients and may take longer than 30 minutes to cook. These recipes have been classified according to the time it takes for them to cook, rather than ease of preparation.

NOTE: Cooking times, oven temperatures and suggested serving sizes on all recipes are a guide only. These will vary slightly depending on ingredients used, oven types and individual cooking techniques.

Disclaimer: *The above symbol means that the ingredients in the recipe are* **either typically gluten-free or can be purchased as gluten-free** *(for example, low-sodium soy sauce and broth/stock).* Please note, some of these products may contain traces of gluten and are therefore not recommended for those with celiac disease. *It is the responsibility of the consumer to always check the ingredients on the manufacturer's labels before consuming their products. This key should be used as a guide only and should not replace any medical advice.*

"Once people understand the cause-and-effect relationship between diet and disease, once they understand the relationship between their dietary and lifestyle choices and the effects on their health and disease, then many will gratefully opt no longer for the good life and its excesses. Instead, they will opt for the best life possible with its elegant simplicity."

[Dr Hans Diehl]

JumpStart

Use these fantastic recipes to get you started on your 5-Day *JumpStart* Challenge. Continue to use these recipes throughout your CHIP journey.

"Fresh fruits and vegetables, rich in color, are simply bursting with life-giving nutrients. Eat a rainbow every day."

[Dr Darren Morton]

5-day JumpStart Challenge

Days 1 and 2
Eat fruit and whole grains.

(Start here if you have diabetes.)

Days 3-5
Eat fruit and whole grains plus vegetables and legumes.

After completing Day 5 of the *JumpStart* Challenge, continue with the *Optimal Diet* principles

Throughout all five days:

❯ Omit refined sugars, honey, molasses and other concentrated sweeteners.

❯ Gradually decrease caffeinated drinks.

❯ Quit all alcohol, fruit juices and soda/soft drinks.

❯ Omit processed fats and oils, including margarine, butter, mayonnaise, oily dressings and vegetable oils.

❯ Avoid processed foods and fast foods.

❯ Leave out animal foods, such as fish, red and white meat.

❯ Leave out dairy products and eggs. Instead of milk, use non-dairy options that are fortified with calcium and B12, such as soy milk or rice milk. If fortified options are not available, or you choose to make your own milk, be sure to include calcium and vitamin B12 supplements in your diet.

❯ Avoid salt. Season with onion, garlic, ginger, herbs and spices, such as cinnamon, cilantro/coriander or cumin.

❯ Avoid eating between meals. When hungry, settle for a glass of water or herbal tea. In emergencies, rely on a piece of fresh fruit.

NOTE: The more thoroughly and conscientiously you implement these principles, the more impressive and convincing will be your benefits.

30 | Complete Health Improvement Program – **EAT MORE**

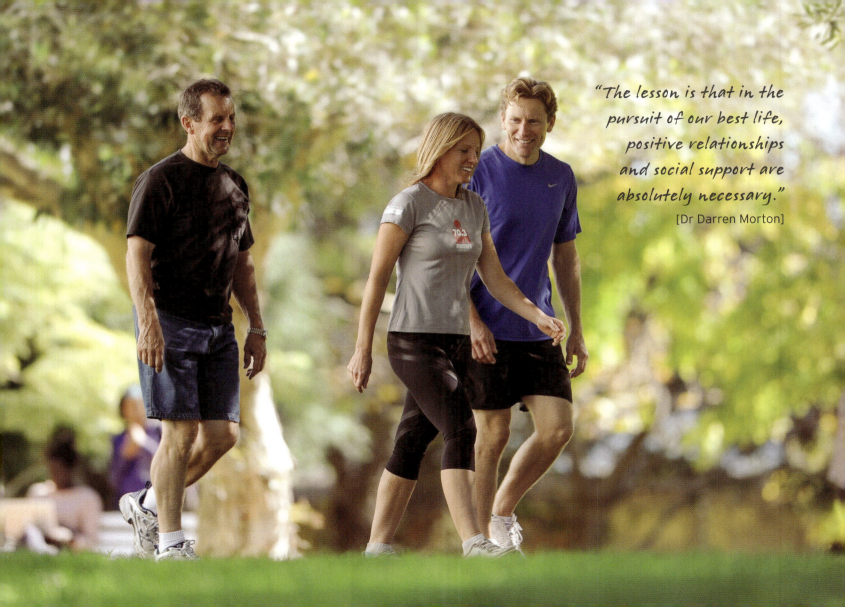

"The lesson is that in the pursuit of our best life, positive relationships and social support are absolutely necessary."

[Dr Darren Morton]

MEAL SUGGESTIONS AND COMBINATIONS–DAYS 1 AND 2

	DAY ONE	DAY TWO
Breakfast	Rolled Oats with dates and cinnamon (page 36) OR Polenta with raisins/sultanas and lemon zest (page 37) + fresh fruit	Whole Wheat or Whole Grain breakfast cereal with dairy-free milk* and fresh fruit OR Berry Oat Smoothie (page 44) + fresh fruit
Lunch	Cooked Brown Rice ADD A variety of fresh or frozen fruit ADD Cinnamon, lemon zest or vanilla if desired or see recipe (page 37)	Cooked Cracked Wheat ADD A variety of fresh or frozen fruit ADD Cinnamon, lemon zest or vanilla if desired or see recipe (page 36)
Supper/Dinner	Cooked Quinoa ADD Your choice of fresh or frozen fruit ADD Cinnamon, lime zest or vanilla if desired or see recipe (page 39)	Cooked Barley ADD Your choice of fresh or frozen fruit ADD Cinnamon, lemon zest or vanilla if desired or see recipe (page 39)

*fortified with calcium and vitamin B12

TIP: For other great combinations of fruits and grains, see *JumpStart* recipes, pages 36-56.

MEAL SUGGESTIONS AND COMBINATIONS–DAYS 3 TO 5

	DAY THREE	DAY FOUR	DAY FIVE
Breakfast	Cornmeal with raisins/sultanas and raspberries (pages 37) OR Whole wheat toast with avocado + Kale and Banana Boost (page 44)	Quick Bircher Muesli (page 62) OR Beet and Berry Blitz (page 44) + fresh fruit	Homemade Baked Beans (page 55) on whole wheat toast OR Apple and Rhubarb with Oat Clusters (page 40)
Lunch	Fennel Citrus Salad (page 43) with whole wheat bread roll and beans of your choice + fresh fruit OR Salad sandwich + Beet and Berry Blitz (page 44)	Baked Potato with beans or Salsa Salad (page 42) + fresh fruit OR Whole wheat pita wrap with fresh salad and Hummus (page 152) + fresh fruit	Chunky Roast Tomato Pasta Salad (page 52) ADD beans if desired + fresh fruit OR Fresh garden salad with your choice of beans and whole wheat bread roll + dried fruit and nuts
Supper/ Dinner	Minestrone Soup (page 51) ADD whole wheat bread roll + fresh fruit OR Lentil and Vegetable Hotpot (page 56) ADD baked potato or brown rice + fresh fruit	Split Pea and Cumin Hotpot (page 48) ADD Whole Wheat bread roll + fresh Fruit OR Black bean and Avocado Salad (page 73) ADD baked potato or whole wheat bread roll + fresh fruit	Lentil and Vegetable Hotpot (page 56) ADD Brown rice or whole wheat pasta + fresh fruit OR Butternut Squash Tagine (page 47) ADD Brown rice or baked potato +fresh fruit

LIVE WELL *JUMPSTART* TIPS:

› Include beans or lentils daily.

› Include at least 2 cups of yellow, green, red and orange raw or cooked vegetables daily.

› Include at least 1 serving of the following per meal:
Starchy vegetables—for example, potato, corn, green peas, sweet potato;
OR
Grains—for example, brown rice, cornmeal/polenta, quinoa, whole wheat pasta.

› Season salads with herbs, non-fat, low-sodium salad dressings or lemon/lime juice.

› In salt-free soups and stews, add extra herbs and spices or sprinkle with salt-substitute seasoning (see page 15).

Be creative, make up your own *JumpStart* meals, or adapt other *Eat More* recipes to suit.

JUMPSTART BREAKFAST RECIPES

Grains	Fruit and Other Ingredients	Preparation	Preparation/ Cooking Times
Rolled Oats	1 cup rolled oats 2½ cups rice milk* 1 teaspoon vanilla extract ¼ teaspoon cinnamon ¼ cup pitted dates, chopped 1 banana, sliced	**1.** Place milk, rolled oats, vanilla extract and cinnamon into a medium saucepan, and stir over a medium heat. Bring to a boil and reduce to simmer. **2.** Add dates and stir through. Continue to cook until oats are tender, stirring occasionally. **3.** Top with sliced banana to serve.	**Preparation time:** 5 minutes **Cooking time:** 25 minutes **Serves:** 2 *Majority of total sugars sourced from whole foods.*
Cracked Wheat	½ cup cracked wheat 2½ cups of rice milk* 2 kiwi fruit, diced ½ cup fresh or frozen blueberries ¼ cup dried apricots, chopped 1 tablespoon chia seeds ½ teaspoon lemon juice ½ teaspoon mixed spice 1 teaspoon vanilla extract	**1.** Place rice milk in a medium saucepan and bring to a boil over medium heat. Add cracked wheat, reduce heat and simmer until milk is absorbed. **2.** Add remaining ingredients, heat and stir through. **3.** Top with additional chopped kiwi fruit, dried apricots and blueberries to serve.	**Preparation time:** 5 minutes **Cooking time:** 25 minutes **Serves:** 2 *Majority of total sugars sourced from whole foods.*

unsweetened, fortified with calcium and vitamin B12

JUMPSTART BREAKFAST RECIPES

Grains	Fruit and Other Ingredients	Preparation	Preparation/ Cooking Times
Brown Rice **GF**	½ cup brown rice 2 cups water 1 cup soy milk* ½ apple, grated ¼ cup raisins/sultanas, chopped 1 medium banana, sliced 1 teaspoon cinnamon	**1.** Place brown rice and water into a medium saucepan and bring to a boil. Reduce heat, cover and simmer until water is absorbed. **2.** Add milk, grated apple, raisins/sultanas, banana and cinnamon. Heat through until warm. **3.** Top with additional sliced banana, grated apple and raisins/sultanas to serve.	**Preparation time:** 5 minutes **Cooking time:** 25 minutes **Serves:** 2 *Majority of total sugars sourced from whole foods.*
Cornmeal/ Polenta **GF**	1 cup cornmeal/polenta 2½ cups rice milk* ½ teaspoon mixed spice 1 teaspoon lemon zest ¼ cup raisins/sultanas ½ cup fresh or frozen raspberries	**1.** Place milk into a medium saucepan and heat over medium heat until almost boiling. Add cornmeal slowly, whisking continually. Turn down heat and continue whisking. **2.** Add mixed spice and lemon zest, and whisk to combine. Add raisins/sultanas and continue stirring over heat for a further 5 minutes. **3.** Top with raspberries or other fruit of your choice to serve.	**Preparation time:** 5 minutes **Cooking time:** 20 minutes **Serves:** 2 *Majority of total sugars sourced from whole foods.*

*unsweetened, fortified with calcium and vitamin B12

TIP: Use these whole grain breakfast recipes throughout your CHIP program. Mix and match any combination of grains and fruit to suit your taste. Make up your own exciting versions of breakfast.

These recipes can be made the night before and kept in the refrigerator overnight. Just heat and serve in the morning and top with fresh fruit of your choice.

For other gluten-free options, try using buckwheat to make your own breakfast grain recipe.

Rolled Oats Nutrient Analysis: PER SERVING: 375 cal (1569kJ); Protein 8g; Total Fat 9g; Saturated Fat 1g; Carbohydrate 61g; Total Sugars 22g; Fiber 10g; Sodium 7mg; Potassium 517mg; Calcium 47mg; Iron 3.5mg; Zinc 1.6mg

Cracked Wheat Nutrient Analysis: PER SERVING: 390 cal (1629kJ); Protein 7g; Total Fat 6g; Saturated Fat <1g; Carbohydrate 76g; Total Sugars 32g; Fiber 10g; Sodium 207mg; Potassium 574mg; Calcium 420mg; Iron 1.7mg

Brown Rice Nutrient Analysis: PER SERVING: 368 cal (1538kJ); Protein 8g; Total Fat 5g; Saturated Fat <1g; Carbohydrate 72g; Total Sugars 24g; Fiber 6g; Sodium 117mg; Potassium 705mg; Calcium 188mg; Iron 2.3mg; Zinc 1.8mg

Cornmeal/Polenta Nutrient Analysis: PER SERVING: 507 cal (2121kJ); Protein 8g; Total Fat 5g; Saturated Fat <1g; Carbohydrate 105g; Total Sugars 31g; Fiber 5g; Sodium 203mg; Potassium 351mg; Calcium 404mg; Iron 1.3mg

Quinoa Nutrient Analysis: PER SERVING: 531 cal (2220kJ); Protein 12g; Total Fat 7g; Saturated Fat <1g; Carbohydrate 101g; Total Sugars 34g; Fiber 7g; Sodium 183mg; Potassium 817mg; Calcium 374mg; Iron 7.7mg; Zinc 2.7mg

Barley Nutrient Analysis: PER SERVING: 469 cal (1961kJ); Protein 14g; Total Fat 5g; Saturated Fat <1g; Carbohydrate 80g; Total Sugars 21g; Fiber 23g; Sodium 21mg; Potassium 780mg; Calcium 78mg; Iron 5.0mg; Zinc 3.3mg

JUMPSTART BREAKFAST RECIPES

Grains	Fruit and Other Ingredients	Preparation	Preparation/ Cooking Times
Quinoa 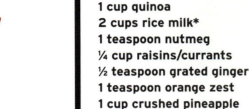	1 cup quinoa 2 cups rice milk* 1 teaspoon nutmeg ¼ cup raisins/currants ½ teaspoon grated ginger 1 teaspoon orange zest 1 cup crushed pineapple	**1.** Place milk and quinoa into a medium saucepan and bring to a boil over medium heat. Reduce heat to simmer, cover and cook until all milk is absorbed. **2.** Add nutmeg, raisins/currants, ginger, orange zest and stir to combine. **3.** Add crushed pineapple just before serving and stir through. **4.** Top with additional crushed pineapple and raisins/currants to serve.	**Preparation time:** 5 minutes **Cooking time:** 25 minutes **Serves:** 2 *Majority of total sugars sourced from whole foods.*
Pearl Barley	1 cup barley 3 cups water 1 cup oat milk* ¼ cup raisins/sultanas ½ teaspoon nutmeg 1 tablespoon lime juice 1 teaspoon lemon zest ½ cup fresh or frozen raspberries	**1.** Place barley and water into a medium saucepan and bring to a boil. Reduce heat, cover and simmer for 35 minutes. When ready, drain water from saucepan. **2.** Add milk, raisins/sultanas, nutmeg, lime juice, lemon zest and raspberries. Heat and stir through. **3.** Top with additional raisins/sultanas and raspberries to serve.	**Preparation time:** 10 minutes **Cooking time:** 50 minutes **Serves:** 2 *Majority of total sugars sourced from whole foods.*

*unsweetened, fortified with calcium and vitamin B12

Apple and Rhubarb with Oat Clusters

Preparation time: 20 minutes **Cooking time:** 20 minutes **Serves:** 8

Apple and Rhubarb Filling

3 large sweet apples, cut into pieces
¼ cup raisins/sultanas, chopped
1 bunch (about 5 stalks) rhubarb, green leaves removed, stalks cut into 1-inch/ 2.5-centimeter pieces
1 cinnamon stick
3 whole cloves
½ cup water
¾ cup apple sauce (unsweetened)

Oat Clusters

2 cups rolled oats
½ cup apple sauce (unsweetened)
⅓ teaspoon cinnamon

1. Preheat oven to 350°F/175°C. Prepare cluster mix by combining rolled oats, apple sauce and cinnamon together and mix well. Spread cluster mixture on a lined baking tray and bake in the oven for 20 minutes or until dry, golden and crispy (stirring occasionally).

2. In a saucepan, combine apple, raisins/sultanas, rhubarb, cinnamon stick and cloves. Add ½ cup of water and bring to a boil on the stove top. Once boiling, turn heat down and simmer, stirring occasionally for 10 minutes or until fruit is soft. Stir through apple sauce and add additional water, if necessary.

3. To serve, remove cinnamon stick and cloves from apple and rhubarb mix, and pour into a serving dish. Top with cluster mix and serve immediately.

Majority of total sugars sourced from whole foods.

Nutrient Analysis: PER SERVING: 205 cal (858kJ); Protein 4g; Total Fat 2g; Saturated Fat <1g; Carbohydrate 38g; Total Sugars 23g; Fiber 6g; Sodium 15mg; Potassium 292mg; Calcium 39mg; Iron 1.5mg

SERVING SUGGESTION: *Sprinkle with chia seeds or nuts.*

Salsa Salad

Preparation time: 15 minutes **Serves:** 4

15 oz/420g can corn kernels, drained and rinsed
1 medium tomato, finely diced
1 medium green bell pepper/capsicum, finely diced
1 medium red bell pepper/capsicum, finely diced
1 small cucumber, finely diced
1 avocado, diced
1 small red onion, finely diced
1 teaspoon ground cumin
1 tablespoon chopped fresh cilantro/coriander
2 tablespoons lime juice

1. Place all ingredients in a bowl and mix together until well combined.

SERVING SUGGESTION: Serve with baked potato and beans, or with tortillas.

Nutrient Analysis: PER SERVING: 211 cal (884kJ); Protein 5g; Total Fat 14g; Saturated Fat 3g; Carbohydrate 14g; Total Sugars 6g; Fiber 6g; Sodium 165mg; Potassium 668mg; Calcium 37mg; Iron 1.4mg; Zinc 1.1mg

Fennel Citrus Salad

Preparation time: 15 minutes **Serves:** 4

1 medium fennel bulb, washed, trimmed and sliced finely
1 grapefruit, peeled and sliced
2 oranges, peeled and sliced
¼ cup dried cranberries

1. Toss all ingredients together and serve.

SERVING SUGGESTION: *Serve with whole grain bread roll and beans of your choice.*

Nutrient Analysis: PER SERVING: 92 cal (386kJ); Protein 2g; Total Fat <1g; Saturated Fat <1g; Carbohydrate 18g; Total Sugars 18g; Fiber 4g; Sodium 26mg; Potassium 356mg; Calcium 47mg

Recipe kindly provided by the Itasca CHIP Chapter, Minnesota, USA.

Berry Oat Smoothie

Preparation time: 10 minutes
Serves: 2

1½ cups rice milk fortified with calcium/B12
½ cup uncooked rolled oats
2 ripe bananas, cut into chunks
½ teaspoon vanilla extract
½ cup frozen mixed berries
1½ tablespoons chia seeds

1. Combine all ingredients in a blender.

2. Blend until smooth and serve immediately.

TIP: *Use frozen bananas for an icy cold and thick smoothie. Serve with fresh berries and mint.*

Majority of total sugars sourced from whole foods.

Nutrient Analysis: PER SERVING: 351 cal (1466kJ); Protein 8g; Total Fat 7g; Saturated Fat <1g; Carbohydrate 65g; Total Sugars 26g; Fiber 10g; Sodium 119mg; Potassium 471mg; Calcium 248mg; Iron 1.3mg

 Rating for all three recipes.

Beet and Blueberry Blitz (GF)

Preparation time: 10 minutes
Serves: 3-4

1 cup raw beets/beetroot, diced
1 cup frozen blueberries
2 teaspoons grated fresh ginger
2 cups seedless grapes, stems removed
1 cup ice
⅔ cup water
1 teaspoon honey

1. Place all ingredients in a blender, blend on high until well combined.

2. Serve immediately.

TIP: *A drink rich in color and full of antioxidants. Serve with muesli for a complete breakfast option.*

Majority of total sugars sourced from whole foods.

Nutrient Analysis: PER SERVING: 99 cal (413kJ); Protein 1g; Total Fat <1g; Saturated Fat <1g; Carbohydrate 22g; Total Sugars 21g; Fiber 4g; Sodium 21mg; Potassium 313mg; Calcium 16mg

Kale and Banana Boost (GF)

Preparation time: 10 minutes
Serves: 3-4

1½ cups crushed pineapple in natural juice
4 frozen medium bananas
1 cup ice
1½ cups shredded kale
¾ cup water
½ lime, juiced
½ lemon, juiced
1 tablespoon grated fresh ginger
2 tablespoons honey

1. Place all ingredients in a blender and process until smooth. Serve chilled.

TIP: *Serve with whole grain bread roll for breakfast.*

Majority of total sugars sourced from whole foods.

Nutrient Analysis: PER SERVING: 193 cal (805kJ); Protein 2g; Total Fat <1g; Saturated Fat <1g; Carbohydrate 43g; Total Sugars 40g; Fiber 4g; Sodium 12mg; Potassium 573mg; Calcium 21mg

Butternut Squash Tagine

Preparation time: 20-30 minutes **Cooking time:** 35 minutes **Serves:** 6

GF

3 tablespoons water
1 onion, finely chopped
3 garlic cloves, crushed
1 teaspoon ground cumin
1 teaspoon ground curry powder/garam masala
1 teaspoon ground coriander
¼ teaspoon chili powder
15 oz/420g can low-sodium diced tomatoes
(or 5 fresh tomatoes, diced)
1 tablespoon no-added-salt tomato paste
¼ cup flat-leaf parsley, chopped
¼ cup cilantro/coriander leaves, chopped
1 can brown lentils, drained and rinsed
or 1¾ cups cooked brown lentils
1.5 lb/600g butternut squash/pumpkin, seeded
and chopped into 1-inch/2.5-centimeter pieces
1 tablespoon raisins/currants (optional)
1 tablespoon sliced almonds (optional)

1. Heat water in a large saucepan, add the onion, and cook over low heat until soft and starting to brown (about 8-10 minutes). Add the garlic and cook for a few seconds, then stir in the ground spices. Cook for 30 seconds, add the tomatoes, tomato paste, and half the parsley and cilantro.

2. Add the lentils and chopped squash/pumpkin. Stir well, then cover and simmer for 20-25 minutes or until the squash is tender.

3. Sprinkle with remaining parsley and cilantro to serve. Top with raisins/currants and almonds (optional).

SERVING SUGGESTION:

Serve with brown rice, couscous or quinoa and baby spinach.

Nutrient Analysis: PER SERVING: 135 cal (565kJ); Protein 8g; Total Fat 2g; Saturated Fat <1g; Carbohydrate 18g; Total Sugars 12g; Fiber 7g; Sodium 24mg; Potassium 905mg; Calcium 62mg; Iron 2.4mg; Zinc 1.2mg

Complete Health Improvement Program – **EAT MORE** | 47

(GF) Split Pea and Cumin Hotpot

Preparation time: 15-20 minutes **Cooking time:** 1 hour **Serves:** 4

1 tablespoon water
1 medium onion, finely chopped
1½ cups yellow split peas, washed
4 cups water
1 large potato, diced
1 large carrot, diced
1 cup celery, diced
2 teaspoons cumin

1. Add water and onion to saucepan and sauté over low heat until transparent.

2. Add yellow split peas and additional water. Cover and bring to a boil. Reduce heat and simmer, stirring occasionally for 35 minutes or until the split peas are soft.

3. Add potatoes, carrot, celery and cumin. Bring back to a boil, reduce heat and simmer until vegetables are tender. Add additional water and salt-substitute seasoning, as needed.

SERVING SUGGESTION:

Serve with whole grain bread roll and fresh fruit.

Nutrient Analysis: PER SERVING: 291 cal (1217kJ); Protein 20g; Total Fat 2g; Saturated Fat <1g; Carbohydrate 45g; Total Sugars 5g; Fiber 10g; Sodium 49mg; Potassium 1054mg; Calcium 71mg; Iron 3.8mg; Zinc 2.3mg

48 | Complete Health Improvement Program – **EAT MORE**

SERVING SUGGESTION: Serve with a warm whole grain bread roll.

Minestrone Soup

Preparation time: 30 minutes **Cooking time:** 40 minutes **Serves:** 8-10

¼ **cup water**
1 **large onion, diced**
3 **cloves garlic, crushed**
5 **cups water**
3 **stalks of celery, diced**
1 **large potato, diced**
4 **medium carrots, diced**
6 **large tomatoes, diced**
8 **medium mushrooms, diced**
2 **bay leaves**
2 **sprigs of fresh rosemary**
½ **cup no-added-salt tomato paste**
15 **oz/420g can no-added-salt condensed tomato soup**
1 **cup whole wheat pasta shapes**
1 **cup sliced green beans, fresh or frozen**
3 **large leaves of Swiss chard/ silverbeet or spinach, shredded**

1. Heat saucepan over low heat. Sauté onion and garlic in a ¼ cup of water, for approximately 5 minutes or until soft.

2. Add 5 cups of water, celery, potato, carrots, tomatoes, mushrooms, bay leaves, rosemary, tomato paste and tomato soup. Increase heat and simmer for about 20 minutes.

3. Add pasta and cook for another 10 minutes.

4. Add beans and chard, and cook for 5 minutes.

5. Add salt-substitute seasoning, if desired, and stir through.

Nutrient Analysis: PER SERVING: 87 cal (364kJ); Protein 4g; Total Fat <1g; Saturated Fat <1g; Carbohydrate 13g; Total Sugars 8g; Fiber 5g; Sodium 168mg; Potassium 759mg; Calcium 66mg; Iron 1.8mg

Pesto

Makes: ¼ cup

- 1 cup basil leaves
- ¼ cup pine nuts
- 1 teaspoon lemon juice
- 2 garlic cloves
- 2 tablespoons sundried tomatoes (not in oil)

1. Combine all ingredients together in a food processor and blend until well combined.

Chunky Roast Tomato Pasta Salad

Preparation time: 15-20 minutes **Cooking time:** 20 minutes **Serves:** 6

Pasta Salad

- 3.5 lb/1.5kg tomatoes, cut into 1-inch/2.5-centimeter cubes
- 1 medium red onion, halved and finely sliced
- ¼ cup pine nuts (optional)
- 4 cloves garlic, finely chopped
- 7 oz/200g whole wheat pasta
- 4 oz/100g baby spinach leaves
- ½ cup small fresh basil leaves
- 2 tablespoons no-added-salt tomato paste
- ⅓ cup sundried tomatoes (not in oil), sliced

1. Preheat oven to 425°F/220°C. Place tomatoes, onion, garlic and pine nuts together on an oven tray. Gently toss to combine. Roast, tossing once, for 20 minutes or until tomatoes are tender.

2. Meanwhile, cook the pasta in plenty of boiling water according to package directions.

3. Drain pasta and return to pan. Stir in pesto, add spinach and toss until spinach begins to wilt. Gently mix in roasted tomatoes, basil, tomato paste and sundried tomatoes. Serve warm.

Nutrient Analysis: PER SERVING: 292 cal (1219kJ); Protein 11g; Total Fat 12g; Saturated Fat <1g; Carbohydrate 30g; Total Sugars 10g; Fiber 11g; Sodium 43mg; Potassium 1245mg; Calcium 99mg; Iron 4.4mg; Zinc 3.5mg

TIP: *Add kidney beans or lentils and sprinkle with extra pine nuts as desired.*

SERVING SUGGESTION:
Serve with a toasted whole grain bread roll.

GF *Homemade Baked Beans*

Preparation time: 20 minutes **Cooking time:** 40 minutes **Serves:** 6

2 teaspoons water
1 medium onion
3 cloves garlic
1 large red bell pepper/capsicum
2 bay leaves
1½ tablespoons coriander seeds
1½ tablespoons paprika
10 thyme sprigs
22 oz/680g jar pureed tomatoes
15 oz/420g can lima/butter beans, drained and rinsed
15 oz/420g can cannellini beans, drained and rinsed

1. Heat water in a medium saucepan, add onion and garlic, and sauté until soft.

2. Add bell pepper, bay leaves, coriander, paprika and thyme. Cook through for 5 minutes until bell pepper is soft.

3. Reduce heat to medium-low, add pureed tomatoes and drained beans, and cook on low heat, stirring occasionally for 30 minutes.

4. Serve with a thick slice of toasted whole wheat bread.

Majority of total sugars sourced from whole foods.

Nutrient Analysis: PER SERVING: 98 cal (408kJ); Protein 6g; Total Fat 1g; Saturated Fat <1 g; Carbohydrate 13g; Total Sugars 21g; Fiber 6g; Sodium 181mg; Potassium 275mg; Calcium 51mg; Iron 1.9mg; Zinc 1.0mg

GF ⏱ *Lentil and Vegetable Hotpot*

Preparation time: 15 minutes **Cooking time:** 60 minutes **Serves:** 6

2 tablespoons water
1 onion, chopped
1 carrot, chopped
6 baby potatoes, quartered
1 lb/450g sweet potatoes, peeled and cubed
4 medium fresh tomatoes, diced
1¾ cups cooked or canned brown lentils
3 tablespoons no-added-salt tomato paste
3 cups water
7 oz/200g green beans, sliced
parsley to serve

1. Heat water in a large saucepan and sauté onion until soft.

2. Add carrot, potato and sweet potatoes, and sauté for 1 minute.

3. Stir through tomatoes, lentils, tomato paste and water. Bring to a boil, then reduce heat and simmer for 45 minutes or until vegetables are cooked.

4. Add beans and cook for 5 more minutes or until tender. Sprinkle with chopped parsley.

5. Serve over couscous or brown rice.

SERVING SUGGESTION:

Serve with a mixed green salad or soy and flax seed bread roll.

Nutrient Analysis: PER SERVING: 197 cal (824kJ); Protein 9g; Total Fat <1g; Saturated Fat <1g; Carbohydrate 34g; Total Sugars 11g; Fiber 8g; Sodium 37mg; Potassium 1283mg; Calcium 72mg; Iron 2.7mg; Zinc 1.7mg

"The foods you include in your diet are as important as the foods you leave out."

[Dr Darren Morton]

Breakfast

Hearty breakfast foods for you to enjoy. Create your own tasty combination of breakfast delights.

....

"One of the important lessons of today is the concept that it's not the amount of food you eat, it's how densely the calories are packed."

[Dr Hans Diehl]

....

Eat More

Wholesome Banana Pancakes

Preparation time: 10 minutes **Cooking time:** 20-30 minutes **Serves:** 7

3 teaspoons egg replacer
1½ tablespoons water
1½ cups plant-based milk (rice or soy)
fortified with calcium/B12
1 cup plain whole wheat flour, sifted
2 teaspoons baking powder
½ cup self-raising flour, sifted
1 teaspoon vanilla extract
1 large or 2 small ripe bananas
1 tablespoon oil

1. Place egg replacer and water in a bowl, and whisk together until smooth. Add rice milk, whole wheat flour and baking powder, whisking after each addition until smooth.

2. Add self-raising flour and vanilla extract to mixture, and continue to whisk until smooth.

3. Mash bananas with a fork and mix through the pancake batter until well combined.

4. Heat a non-stick skillet or frying pan, using a non-stick cooking spray, if needed.

5. Fry ¼ cup of batter in a hot pan until bottom is golden brown. Turn with spatula and cook to brown the other side. Repeat with remaining mixture.

6. Serve hot with your choice of healthy toppings.

Nutrient Analysis: PER SERVING: 171 cal (713kJ); Protein 4g; Total Fat 2g; Saturated Fat <1g; Carbohydrate 32g; Total Sugars 5g; Fiber 2g; Sodium 365mg; Potassium 120mg; Calcium 76mg

SERVING SUGGESTION: *Top with your favorite fresh seasonal fruit and Sweet Cashew Cream (see page 149).*

VARIATION: For a creamy option, add ¼ cup light coconut milk or nut cream, such as Sweet Cashew Cream (see page 149).

Quick Bircher Muesli with Chia

Preparation time: 5 minutes
Soaking time: 10-15 mins **Serves:** 2

1 cup rolled oats
1 cup orange juice
1 tablespoon lemon juice
1 apple, cored and grated
¼ teaspoon cinnamon
1 tablespoon chia seeds

1. Combine oats with orange juice, lemon juice and grated apple, and allow to soak for 10-15 minutes.

2. Sprinkle with cinnamon and chia seeds, and serve with fresh fruit of your choice, such as strawberries, raspberries, peaches, figs, blueberries, banana or cherries.

TIP: *This can be made the evening before. Combine oats with orange juice, lemon juice and cinnamon and soak overnight. Add grated apple, chia seeds and other fresh fruit in the morning for a tasty breakfast.*

Majority of total sugars sourced from whole foods.

Nutrient Analysis: PER SERVING: 306 cal (1278kJ); Protein 8g; Total Fat 6g; Saturated Fat <1g; Carbohydrate 53g; Total Sugars 22g; Fiber 9g; Sodium 13mg; Potassium 456mg; Calcium 42mg; Iron 2.2mg; Zinc 1.3mg

Oat and Cashew Waffles

Preparation time: 10 minutes
Cooking time: 10-12 minutes per waffle **Makes:** 5 waffles

2 cups water
1½ cups rolled oats
⅓ cup raw cashews
½ teaspoon salt (optional)

1. Place all ingredients in a food processor or blender, and mix until well combined and slightly thickened.

2. Fill waffle maker to the desired level, close the lid and allow to cook for 10-12 minutes. Do not open the lid before it is finished, as waffles may tear apart.

3. Serve hot or cold, with your favorite fresh berries and other seasonal fruit.

TIPS: *Waffles may be covered and frozen for use at a later date.*

For sweet waffles, add a couple of dates and a teaspoon of vanilla extract to step 1 (soften the dates in boiling water for a few minutes before adding).

Nutrient Analysis: PER SERVING: 159 cal (664kJ); Protein 5g; Total Fat 7g; Saturated Fat 1g; Carbohydrate 18g; Total Sugars <1g; Fiber 3g; Sodium 240mg; Potassium 138mg; Calcium 17mg; Iron 1.5mg; Zinc 1.0mg

Potato Rosti

Preparation time: 10 minutes **Cooking time:** 40 minutes **Serves:** 6

1 lb/500g washed potatoes, with skins
½ **tablespoon almond butter**
½ **teaspoon salt (optional)**
¼ **teaspoon garlic powder**
½ **teaspoon onion powder**
2 **tablespoons chopped parsley**

1. Place washed potatoes in a saucepan. Add enough water to completely cover the potatoes. Cook until still slightly firm. Remove from heat, cool, then grate the potato.

2. Preheat oven to 350°F/180°C with broil/grill setting on. Combine grated potato with almond butter, salt and seasonings, and form into patties.

3. Place patties on a cookie sheet/tray that has been lightly sprayed with non-stick cooking spray. Put sheet/tray under broil/grill element for 6-8 minutes, turn patties, and broil for 6-8 more minutes or until lightly browned. Serve hot.

SERVING SUGGESTION:

Serve with baked beans and sautéed vegetables.

Nutrient Analysis: PER SERVING: 67 cal (281kJ); Protein 2g; Total Fat 1g; Saturated Fat <1g; Carbohydrate 11g; Total Sugars <1g; Fiber 2g; Sodium 202mg; Potassium 437mg; Calcium 9mg

Creamy Mushrooms

Preparation time: 15 minutes **Cooking time:** 15 minutes **Serves:** 6

1 tablespoon oil
1 medium onion, halved and sliced
2 cloves garlic, finely diced
1 lb/500g mushrooms, sliced
5.5 oz/165ml can light coconut milk
3 oz/75g baby spinach

1. Heat oil in a medium skillet or frying pan. Add onion and garlic, and sauté until soft.

2. Add sliced mushrooms and cook until browned, stirring occasionally. Add coconut milk, heat through, then add baby spinach and serve.

SERVING SUGGESTION:

Serve mushrooms with toasted whole wheat bread. This will add extra fiber to your meal.

Nutrient Analysis: PER SERVING: 100 cal (420kJ); Protein 4g; Total Fat 8g; Saturated Fat 4g; Carbohydrate 3g; Total Sugars 2g; Fiber 2g; Sodium 18mg; Potassium 445mg; Calcium 18mg; Iron 1.1mg

TIP: *Refrigerate mushrooms in a brown paper bag. Mushrooms stored in plastic bags will sweat and deteriorate.*

"Eating more plant-based meals is a good recipe for our own health and that of the planet. Diets dominated by whole grains, legumes, nuts, seeds, fruits and vegetables are almost certainly the way of the future."
[Dr Rosemary Stanton]

Salads and Vegetables

Fresh and tasty salads and vegetables bursting with color to brighten your day.
Combine with your choice of main or light meal options for a more substantial meal.

"Attitudes toward vegetarian diets have progressed from ridicule and skepticism to condescending tolerance, to gradual and sometimes grudging acceptance, and finally to acclaim."

[Dr Mervyn Hardinge]

Eat More

Kale and Beet Salad

Preparation time: 15 minutes **Serves:** 6

Salad
2 carrots, peeled and grated
2 fresh beets/beetroots, peeled and grated
1 zucchini, grated
8 kale leaves, finely shredded
⅓ cup pumpkin seeds/pepitas, roasted

Dressing
¼ cup lemon juice
1 tablespoon honey
pinch of salt (optional)

TIP:
Top with parsley to give some extra flavor.

1. Combine carrots, beets, zucchini and shredded kale leaves in a bowl, and mix gently.

Dressing
1. Place lemon juice, honey and salt in a small sealed container, and shake well to combine. Pour over salad and mix through.

2. Toss roasted pepitas through, just before serving.

Nutrient Analysis: PER SERVING: 85 cal (356kJ); Protein 3g; Total Fat 4g; Saturated Fat <1g; Carbohydrate 8g; Total Sugars 8g; Fiber 3g; Sodium 87mg; Potassium 255mg; Calcium 24mg

VARIATION: Use red kidney beans or any other beans of your choice in place of black beans.

Black Bean and Avocado Salad

Preparation time: 15 minutes **Serves:** 6-8

3 cups cooked black beans
3 cups corn kernels
½ cup red onion, thinly sliced
¼ cup finely chopped cilantro/coriander
¼ teaspoon garlic powder
1 lime, juiced
1 lemon, juiced
2 large avocados, cubed

1. In a large bowl, combine black beans, corn kernels, red onion, cilantro, garlic powder, lime juice, lemon juice and avocado. Toss gently to combine.

2. Serve chilled.

Recipe kindly provided by Capital City CHIP Chapter, Alaska, USA.

Nutrient Analysis: PER SERVING: 265 cal (1107kJ); Protein 9g; Total Fat 14g; Saturated Fat 3g; Carbohydrate 21g; Total Sugars 4g; Fiber 9g; Sodium 165mg; Potassium 649mg; Calcium 32mg; Iron 2.2mg; Zinc 1.5mg

Garden Rice Salad

Preparation time: 30 minutes **Cooking time:** 40 minutes **Serves:** 12

Salad
- 5 cups cooked brown rice
- 9 oz/250g cherry tomatoes, cut into quarters
- 1 small cucumber, finely diced
- ½ red bell pepper/capsicum, finely diced
- ½ green bell pepper/capsicum, finely diced
- 7 oz/200g jar kalamata olives, drained and diced
- 15 oz/400g can no-added-salt beans of your choice, drained and rinsed
- 15 oz/420g can no-added-salt corn kernels, drained and rinsed
- 1 bunch of chives, chopped
- ½ cup almonds, roasted

Dressing
- 1 tablespoon oil
- 1½ tablespoons honey
- 3 tablespoons lemon juice
- 1½ teaspoons low-sodium tamari or soy sauce (GF)

TIP: *Great dish to serve when entertaining guests.*

1. Cook brown rice according to instructions on package and let it cool.

2. Place brown rice, tomatoes, cucumber, bell peppers, olives, beans of choice, corn kernels, chives and almonds into a bowl, and mix until well combined. Leave aside a small amount of vegetables for garnish.

Dressing
1. Place oil, honey, lemon juice and tamari or soy sauce in a small sealed container, and shake until well combined.

2. Drizzle dressing over salad and serve immediately.

Nutrient Analysis: PER SERVING: 257 cal (1073kJ); Protein 6g; Total Fat 8g; Saturated Fat <1g; Carbohydrate 38g; Total Sugars 6g; Fiber 5g; Sodium 333mg; Potassium 262mg; Calcium 43mg; Iron 1.6mg; Zinc 1.4mg

Potato and Corn Salad

Preparation time: 15 minutes
Cooking time: 20 minutes **Serves:** 6

6 small potatoes, cut in quarters
1 sweet potato, diced
1 cup low-sodium corn kernels, drained and rinsed
½ red onion, diced
1 tablespoon parsley, chopped
½ cup eggless mayonnaise (see page 146)
½ teaspoon salt (optional)

1. Steam baby potatoes and sweet potato until tender. Set aside to cool.

2. In a bowl, combine corn kernels, red onion, parsley and mayonnaise. Add cooled potato and sweet potato, and stir until all ingredients are evenly coated with mayonnaise.

3. Season with salt or your favorite salt-free seasoning.

TIP: *Keep the skin on your potatoes. This will help the potatoes retain their shape during cooking.*

Nutrient Analysis: PER SERVING: 161 cal (673kJ); Protein 4g; Total Fat 4g; Saturated Fat <1g; Carbohydrate 25g; Total Sugars 5g; Fiber 4g; Sodium 219mg; Potassium 688mg; Calcium 21mg; Iron 1.0mg

SERVING SUGGESTION: Serve salad with a falafel in a whole wheat pita wrap, or with Corn and Pea Fritters (see page 113) for a complete meal.

GF ⏱ *Cucumber and Dill Salad*

Preparation time: 20 minutes **Serves:** 6-8

Salad

**3 small cucumbers, cut in half
lengthways and thinly sliced
1 zucchini, grated
½ red bell pepper/capsicum, diced
2 tablespoons sesame seeds, roasted
1 teaspoon fresh dill
1 teaspoon salt (optional)**

Dressing

**2 limes, juiced
1 tablespoon honey
½ teaspoon grated fresh ginger
1 teaspoon salt (optional)**

1. Place sliced cucumber in mixing bowl. Add zucchini, red pepper, sesame seeds, dill and salt.

2. Mix gently to combine.

Dressing

1. Place lime juice, honey, ginger and salt into a sealed container, and shake to combine.

2. Drizzle over the salad and serve immediately.

Nutrient Analysis: PER SERVING: 37 cal (155kJ); Protein 1g; Total Fat 2g; Saturated Fat <1g; Carbohydrate 4g; Total Sugars 4g; Fiber 1g; Sodium 305mg; Potassium 81mg; Calcium 27mg

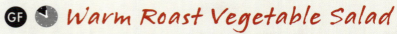

Warm Roast Vegetable Salad

Preparation time: 20 minutes **Cooking time:** 40 minutes **Serves:** 6

Dressing
2 tablespoons honey
1½ tablespoons low-sodium tamari (GF)
2 tablespoons lemon juice

1. Place all dressing ingredients in a sealed container and shake until well combined.

2. When ready, drizzle vegetables evenly with dressing, and garnish with fresh herbs of your choice. Serve warm.

Majority of total sugars sourced from whole foods.

Roast Vegetables
1 red bell pepper/capsicum, cut in half, seeds removed
1-2 eggplant/aubergine, cut into ½-inch/1.5-centimeter slices
2 lb/800g pumpkin or butternut squash, peeled and diced (2-centimeter-thick chunks)
6 small beets/beetroot, peeled and cut into wedges
6 small washed potatoes, cut in half
6 small onions, cut in quarters
1 bunch asparagus

Nutrient Analysis: PER SERVING: 211 cal (883kJ); Protein 8g; Total Fat 1g; Saturated Fat <1g; Carbohydrate 37g; Total Sugars 26g; Fiber 9g; Sodium 307mg; Potassium 1293mg; Calcium 55mg; Iron 1.9mg; Zinc 1.5mg

1. Preheat oven to 450°F/240°C. Place halved peppers face down on a lightly oiled tray and roast in the oven for 30-40 minutes, or until blackened and sunken.

2. Meanwhile, place eggplant, pumpkin, beets, potatoes and onions on an lightly oiled oven tray in a single layer. Spray lightly with oil and roast vegetables in the oven for approximately 20 minutes, or until lightly browned and cooked in the middle.

3. When bell peppers are ready, remove from oven, place in a bowl, cover with plastic wrap, and allow to cool. When cool, remove skin from bell peppers, and cut into chunky slices about 1 inch/2.5 centimeters thick.

4. Place asparagus in boiling water and cook for 2-5 minutes or until a vibrant green color.

5. Remove all vegetables from the oven when done, and allow to cool slightly.

6. Combine all vegetables together and place on a serving dish.

TIP: Some vegetables, such as potatoes, may take longer to cook than the other vegetables, depending on their size.

GF ⏱ Cabbage and Pineapple Salad

Preparation time: 15-20 minutes **Cooking time:** 20 minutes **Serves:** 6

Salad

1½ cups pineapple pieces
5 cups shredded red or white cabbage
1 carrot, julienned
½ red bell pepper/capsicum, diced
¼ cup flat-leaf parsley, finely sliced

Dressing

1 tablespoon lemon juice
2 tablespoons pineapple juice
4 tablespoons sesame seeds, toasted
½ teaspoon sesame oil
1 teaspoon honey
⅛ teaspoon salt (optional)

TIP:

Can be made ahead and kept in fridge. Add dressing when ready to serve.

1. Drain juice from canned pineapple into a separate container, and set aside for use in dressing.

2. Place cabbage, pineapple pieces, carrot, red pepper and parsley in a bowl. Mix well to combine.

Dressing

1. Place lemon juice, pineapple juice, sesame seeds, sesame oil, honey and salt (optional) in a small sealed container. Shake well to combine.

2. Just before serving, coat salad with dressing and toss gently to combine.

Nutrient Analysis: PER SERVING: 101 cal (421kJ); Protein 4g; Total Fat 5g; Saturated Fat <1g; Carbohydrate 8g; Total Sugars 8g; Fiber 5g; Sodium 70mg; Potassium 505mg; Calcium 48mg; iron 1.1mg

Quinoa and Fig Salad with Lemon Dressing

GF

Preparation time: 15 minutes **Cooking time:** 40 minutes **Serves:** 6

Salad

2 red bell peppers/capsicums
1 cup cooked quinoa
3 cups arugula/baby rocket leaves, washed
¼ cup dried figs, finely sliced
½ cup slivered almonds, toasted
zest of 1 orange
flesh of 2 oranges, chopped

Dressing

½ teaspoon grated fresh ginger
½ cup fresh lemon juice
1 tablespoon honey
2 teaspoons lemon zest
½ teaspoon salt (optional)

1. Preheat oven to 475°F/250°C. Cut red bell peppers in half length ways and remove seeds. Place face down on oven tray and roast for 35-40 minutes, or until blackened and sunken. Remove from oven and place into a bowl, cover with plastic wrap and leave to cool.

2. Once cool, peel skin from peppers and slice into thin strips.

3. Combine roasted peppers with cooked quinoa, arugula leaves, figs, almonds, orange zest and oranges. Mix gently to combine.

Dressing

1. Place ginger, lemon juice, honey, lemon zest and salt (optional) into a small sealed container, and shake well to combine.

2. Drizzle dressing over salad and toss gently to serve.

Nutrient Analysis: PER SERVING: 179 cal (748kJ); Protein 5g; Total Fat 7g; Saturated Fat <1g; Carbohydrate 21g; Total Sugars 15g; Fiber 5g; Sodium 211mg; Potassium 473mg; Calcium 77mg; Iron 2.4mg; Zinc 1.2mg

DID YOU KNOW?

Quinoa is rich in high-quality protein, even more than oats.

DID YOU KNOW?
Spinach is an excellent source of iron.

GF Strawberry Spinach Salad

Preparation time: 15 minutes **Cooking time:** 3 minutes **Serves:** 6-8

Salad

½ cup slivered almonds
8 oz/225g baby spinach leaves, washed
9 oz/250g fresh strawberries, washed, tops removed and cut into quarters
1 tablespoon sesame seeds
½ tablespoon poppy seeds

Dressing

1 tablespoon olive oil
2 tablespoons lemon juice
½ tablespoon honey
1 teaspoon low-sodium soy sauce (GF)
1 tablespoon finely sliced fresh mint

1. Preheat oven to 350°F/180°C. Place almonds onto oven tray and bake for 2-3 minutes to toast, checking regularly. Once lightly browned, remove and set aside to cool.

2. Combine spinach leaves, strawberries, toasted almonds, sesame seeds and poppy seeds in a bowl, and toss gently to combine.

Dressing

1. Place olive oil, lemon juice, honey, soy sauce and mint into a small sealed container, and shake well to combine.

2. Drizzle over the salad and serve immediately.

Recipe kindly provided by Beaverton CHIP Chapter, Oregon, USA.

Nutrient Analysis: PER SERVING: 94 cal (391kJ); Protein 3g; Total Fat 7g; Saturated Fat <1g; Carbohydrate 3g; Total Sugars 3g; Fiber 2g; Sodium 35mg; Potassium 361mg; Calcium 48mg; Iron 2.0mg

GF # Arugula, Eggplant and Bean Salad

Preparation time: 20 minutes **Cooking time:** 15 minutes **Serves:** 6-8

Salad

1 aubergine/eggplant, diced
1 sweet potato, diced
6 cloves garlic, whole
1 orange, peeled and sectioned
15 oz/420g can pinto/borlotti beans, drained and rinsed
¼ red onion, thinly sliced
⅓ cup slivered almonds
5 cups arugula/rocket, washed

Dressing

3 tablespoons almond butter
6 tablespoons fresh orange juice
½ teaspoon salt (optional)
1 teaspoon honey
2 teaspoons low-sodium soy sauce (GF)

1. Preheat oven to 475°F/240°C. Place eggplant, sweet potato and garlic cloves on a baking sheet/tray, and roast in the oven for 15 minutes or until well done. Set aside to cool.

2. Place cooled eggplant, sweet potato and garlic in a bowl with orange segments, beans, red onion, arugula and slivered almonds. Mix gently to combine.

Dressing

1. Combine almond butter, orange juice, salt (optional), honey and soy sauce in a small sealed jar or container. Shake well to combine.

2. Drizzle dressing over salad to serve.

Nutrient Analysis: PER SERVING: 141 cal (591kJ); Protein 6g; Total Fat 7g; Saturated Fat <1g; Carbohydrate 11g; Total Sugars 6g; Fiber 5g; Sodium 201mg; Potassium 303mg; Calcium 34mg; Iron 1.0mg; Zinc 1.0mg

SERVING SUGGESTION: *Serve this salad with Lentil and Sesame Rissoles (see page 120) for a complete meal.*

(Peggy West and Lynda Nelson Collection)

VARIATION: *Try adding some toasted, crushed almonds to this dish.*

Sweet Potatoes with Orange Sauce

Preparation time: 15 minutes **Cooking time:** 1 hour 30 minutes **Serves:** 12

4 large sweet potatoes, whole
2 tablespoons cornstarch/arrowroot powder
½ cup cold water
1 cup fresh orange juice
1 cup unsweetened pineapple juice
2 tablespoons honey (optional)
1 teaspoon grated orange peel
¼ teaspoon salt (optional)
¼ cup chopped pecans or unsweetened shredded coconut

1. Preheat oven to 350°F/180°C. Bake sweet potatoes for 1 hour or until tender. Cool and peel. Slice and place in a casserole dish.

2. In a small bowl, add water gradually to cornstarch, stirring constantly to maintain smoothness. Then add orange juice, pineapple juice, honey, orange peel and salt (optional). Mix until well combined and pour over sliced sweet potatoes. Bake in a covered dish until thoroughly heated.

3. Top with chopped pecans or shredded coconut.

Nutrient Analysis: PER SERVING: 93 cal (390kJ); Protein 1g; Total Fat 2g; Saturated Fat <1g; Carbohydrate 17g; Total Sugars 7g; Fiber 2g; Sodium 55mg; Potassium 361mg; Calcium 4mg

Recipe kindly provided by Greeneville CHIP Chapter, Tennessee, USA.

Honey and Ginger Carrots

Preparation time: 10 minutes
Cooking time: 10 minutes **Serves:** 4

6 carrots, peeled and sliced diagonally
2 teaspoons honey
½ tablespoon grated ginger
1 tablespoon chopped parsley (optional)

1. Cook carrots in boiling water until tender, then drain well.

2. Add honey and ginger, toss well. Garnish with chopped parsley, if desired.

DID YOU KNOW? Carrots are high in beta-carotene, from which the body makes vitamin A.

Nutrient Analysis: PER SERVING: 40 cal (169kJ); Protein <1g; Total Fat <1g; Saturated Fat <1g; Carbohydrate 8g; Total Sugars 8g; Fiber 4g; Sodium 37mg; Potassium 263mg; Calcium 29mg

Recipe kindly provided by Apopka CHIP Chapter, Florida, USA.

Kale with Pine Nuts

Preparation time: 15 minutes
Cooking time: 10 minutes **Serves:** 2

1 bunch kale
1 tablespoon olive oil
2 cloves garlic, crushed
2 tablespoons pine nuts, roasted
¼ teaspoon salt (optional)
1 lemon, cut into wedges

1. Strip kale leaves from the stem and shred. Place shredded kale in a large pot of boiling water and blanch for 3-4 minutes, to retain the bright green color. Remove and drain.

2. Heat olive oil in a frying pan and sauté garlic for 1 minute. Add kale and sauté over low heat for 3-5 minutes, stirring frequently.

3. Add pine nuts, salt (optional) and a squeeze of lemon juice and stir-fry for an additional 2 minutes.

4. Serve with a wedge of lemon.

Nutrient Analysis: PER SERVING: 217 cal (909kJ); Protein 4g; Total Fat 20g; Saturated Fat 2g; Carbohydrate 4g; Total Sugars 3g; Fiber 4g; Sodium 318mg; Potassium 451mg; Calcium 46mg; Iron 1.3mg; Zinc 1.1mg

SERVING SUGGESTION: *Serve with Lentil and Sesame Rissoles (see page 120) for a complete meal.*

GF 🕐 *Steamed Vegetables*
with Creamy Cashew White Sauce

Preparation time: 10 minutes **Cooking time:** 10 minutes **Serves:** 6

½ **head of cauliflower,**
broken into florets
½ **head of broccoli,**
broken into florets
1 bunch asparagus
1 cup creamy cashew white
sauce (see page 146)

1. Place cauliflower in a steamer and cook for 5 minutes over boiling water. Add broccoli and asparagus, and steam for an additional 2 minutes or until tender but still bright green.

2. Place steamed vegetables in a serving dish and pour white sauce over vegetables to serve.

TIP: *Broccoli contains phytochemicals which may help protect against many chronic diseases including certain types of cancer.*

Nutrient Analysis: PER SERVING: 97 cal (413kJ); Protein 5g; Total Fat 6g; Saturated Fat 1g; Carbohydrate 4g; Total Sugars 2g; Fiber 4g; Sodium 290mg; Potassium 435mg; Calcium 29mg; Iron 1.4mg; Zinc 1.0mg

Complete Health Improvement Program – **EAT MORE** | 93

Soups

Healthy, heartwarming soups to nourish your soul.
Serve with freshly baked whole grain bread rolls to tempt your tastebuds.

"Let all deprivation diets die. Deprivation diets have no place in a successful long-term strategy."

[Dr Hans Diehl]

Eat More

SERVING SUGGESTION: Serve with a toasted whole grain bread roll.

Potato and Corn Chowder

Preparation time: 15 minutes **Cooking time:** 25 minutes **Serves:** 6

1 large onion, diced, or ¼ cup onion flakes
6 medium potatoes, scrubbed and diced
4 cups water
2 cups whole corn kernels
2 teaspoons low-sodium broth/ stock powder
1 cup raw cashews
1 cup water
chopped parsley or diced scallions/ green onions (to garnish)

1. Place onion and potatoes in water and bring to a boil. Reduce heat and simmer until potatoes are cooked.

2. Add corn and stock, and return to a boil. Meanwhile, blend cashews with 1 cup of water in a blender, until smooth and creamy. When soup comes to a boil, add cashew mix. Rinse blender with a little water and add this to soup.

3. Reduce heat to simmer for a few minutes until heated through. Garnish with parsley or scallions.

Nutrient Analysis: PER SERVING: 300 cal (1254kJ); Protein 10g; Total Fat 13g; Saturated Fat 2g; Carbohydrate 33g; Total Sugars 5g; Fiber 6g; Sodium 288mg; Potassium 967mg; Calcium 25mg; Iron 2.3mg; Zinc 2.2mg

Recipe kindly provided by Rocky Mount CHIP Chapter, Virginia, USA.

GF 🕐 *Roast Pepper and Pumpkin Soup*

Preparation time: 20 minutes **Cooking time:** 60 minutes **Serves:** 4

3 red bell peppers/capsicums
¼ cup water
1 medium onion, chopped
3 cloves of garlic, chopped
2 lb/800g pumpkin, peeled and chopped
2 medium potatoes, peeled and chopped
2 cups water
½ teaspoon salt (optional)
10 basil leaves

1. Preheat oven to 475°F/250°C. Cut bell peppers in half and place face down on tray. Roast peppers until blackened and sunken.

2. Meanwhile, in a large saucepan over medium heat, sauté onion and garlic in ¼ cup water until transparent.

3. Add pumpkin and potato to onion mixture. Cover with water and boil until soft.

4. Remove peppers from oven, place in a bowl and cover with plastic wrap. Allow to cool and sweat. When cool, remove the skin.

5. Add peppers, salt (optional) and basil leaves to soup. Use stick blender or place in blender to blend until smooth and creamy. Hold lid firmly in place while processing hot liquids. Garnish with extra basil leaves and serve hot.

Nutrient Analysis: PER SERVING: 165 cal (691kJ); Protein 6g; Total Fat <1g; Saturated Fat <1g; Carbohydrate 29g; Total Sugars 17g; Fiber 9g; Sodium 306mg; Potassium 1154mg; Calcium 68mg; Iron 1.2mg

VARIATION: *For a creamy version of this soup, add 1 cup of raw cashew nuts pureed with ¾ cup water and ½ teaspoon salt.*

DID YOU KNOW?
Sweet potatoes are an excellent source of minerals such as potassium, iron, copper and magnesium.

Recipe kindly provided by Hood View CHIP Chapter, Oregon, USA.

GF 🕐 *White Bean and Sweet Potato Soup with Greens*

Preparation time: 20 minutes **Cooking time:** 40 minutes **Serves:** 5

¼ **cup water**
1 onion, diced
2 cloves garlic, crushed
1 small red pepper/capsicum, deseeded and diced
1 lb/500g sweet potatoes, cut in 1-inch/2.5-centimeter cubes
1 fresh hot chili, seeded and chopped finely (optional)
1 teaspoon grated fresh ginger
14.5 oz/415g can diced tomatoes
2 x 15 oz/420g cans white beans (cannellini or navy), drained and rinsed
1 teaspoon honey
½ **teaspoon ground allspice**
¼ **teaspoon cumin**
2 bay leaves
3 cups water
2 cups collards or broccoli, chopped

1. Heat water in a large saucepan and sauté onion, garlic and red pepper until soft.

2. Add the sweet potatoes, chili, ginger, tomatoes, beans, honey, allspice, cumin, bay leaves and water. Bring to a boil, reduce heat and cook until sweet potatoes are almost done.

3. Add collards or broccoli and cook until soft. Remove bay leaves before serving.

Nutrient Analysis: PER SERVING: 197 cal (823kJ); Protein 11g; Total Fat 1g; Saturated Fat <1g; Carbohydrate 32g; Total Sugars 13g; Fiber 11g; Sodium 374mg; Potassium 863mg; Calcium 113mg; Iron 3.0mg, Zinc 1.6mg

Green Pea and Cilantro Soup

GF

Preparation time: 5 minutes **Cooking time:** 25 minutes **Serves:** 4

**2 medium potatoes,
peeled and diced
2 cloves garlic, diced
1 medium onion, diced
1 teaspoon salt (optional)
3 cups water
9 oz/250g frozen peas
¼ cup fresh cilantro/coriander
coconut milk to garnish**

1. Place potatoes, garlic, onion, salt (optional) and water in a saucepan. Bring to a boil and cook until vegetables are tender.

2. Add frozen peas and cook for 5 more minutes or until boiling.

3. Remove from heat, add cilantro and blend with a stick blender or in a blender until smooth. Hold lid firmly in place while processing hot liquids.

4. Garnish with a sprig of cilantro and a dash of coconut milk to serve.

Nutrient Analysis: PER SERVING: 90 cal (375kJ); Protein 6g; Total Fat <1g; Saturated Fat <1g; Carbohydrate 13g; Total Sugars 3g; Fiber 6g; Sodium 601mg; Potassium 398mg; Calcium 28mg; Iron 1.5mg; Zinc 1.4mg

VARIATION: *Add fresh mint or use minted peas, if available.*

"The long-lived Okinawans have a saying 'Hara Hachi Bu' which means leave the table when you feel 80 percent full."
[Dan Buettner, *The Blue Zones*]

Light Meals

Delight your tastebuds with these quick and easy light meals.
Great for lunch options at work or school.

"Let's not become enslaved to the scale, because as we begin to eat more and more for health, the scale will increasingly take care of itself."

[Dr Hans Diehl]

Eat More

Tabbouleh Salad
Makes: 4 cups

1 cup cracked wheat
2 cups boiling water
2 medium tomatoes,
  finely diced
1 clove garlic, crushed
1 bunch of parsley, stems
  removed and finely chopped
2 teaspoons lemon juice
½ teaspoon salt (optional)
pinch of chili powder (optional)

1. Place cracked wheat and water into a small saucepan and place on the stove. Bring to a boil, reduce heat and simmer for 15 minutes. Remove from heat, drain water and rinse.

2. Combine cracked wheat, tomatoes, garlic, parsley, lemon juice, salt (optional) and chili powder, and mix until well combined.

Hummus and Tabbouleh Wrap

Preparation time: 20 minutes **Cooking time:** 15 minutes **Serves:** 4

4 whole wheat wraps
½ cup hummus
Tabbouleh Salad
1 cucumber, sliced
4 tomatoes, sliced
½ red onion, sliced

1. Spread one-fourth of the hummus evenly over each wrap, leaving edges bare.

2. In the center of the wrap, place a row of tabbouleh, cucumber, tomato and onion. Fold up one end and roll together to complete wrap. Wrap in baking paper to hold in place.

TIP:

Serve with a squeeze of fresh lemon or lime.

Nutrient Analysis: PER SERVING: 315 cal (1308kJ); Protein 12g; Total Fat 7g; Saturated Fat 2g; Carbohydrate 44g; Total Sugars 9g; Fiber 12g; Sodium 592mg; Potassium 776mg; Calcium 67mg; Iron 2.3mg; Zinc 1.7mg

Cashew Cheese and Salad Pita Pocket

Preparation time: 10 minutes **Makes:** 8 halves **Serves:** 4

4 whole wheat pita pockets
4 large lettuce leaves
1 avocado
6 sundried tomatoes
(not in oil), sliced
1 large carrot, grated
½ cup grated Cashew Cheese
(see page 153)
1 cup alfalfa sprouts

1. Cut pita pockets in half and fill with avocado, lettuce, sundried tomatoes, carrot, cashew cheese and alfalfa sprouts.

2. Serve immediately.

SERVING SUGGESTION:

Serve with fresh seasonal fruit.

Nutrient Analysis: PER SERVING: 366 cal (1528kJ); Protein 10g; Total Fat 17g; Saturated Fat 4g; Carbohydrate 40g; Total Sugars 5g; Fiber 6g; Sodium 402mg; Potassium 746mg; Calcium 40mg; Iron 2.4mg; Zinc 2.2mg

Wrap

Preparation time: 10 minutes
Serves: 4

Wrap

4 whole grain tortilla wraps
1 avocado, halved
4 lettuce leaves
Scrambled Tofu
1 cucumber, sliced
1 carrot, grated
2 tomatoes, sliced
1 cup alfalfa sprouts

1. Spread avocado evenly over the wrap. In the center of the wrap, place a row of lettuce, scrambled tofu, cucumber, carrot, tomato, and alfalfa sprouts. Fold up one end and roll together to complete. Wrap in baking paper to hold together.

Scrambled Tofu and Salad Wrap

Preparation time: 5 minutes **Cooking time:** 15 minutes **Serves:** 4

Scrambled tofu

1 onion, finely diced
2 cloves of garlic, crushed
1 tablespoon oil
12 oz/320g firm tofu, mashed
2 teaspoons onion powder
½ teaspoon garlic powder
¼ teaspoon turmeric
½ teaspoon curry powder
½ teaspoon salt (optional)
½ cup Eggless Mayonnaise (see page 146)
1 tablespoon chopped parsley

1. Sauté onion and garlic in oil until soft.

2. Add tofu, spices and salt, and continue cooking on low/medium heat until scrambled. Add mayonnaise and stir through.

3. Add parsley and remove from heat. Spread out on tray and set aside to cool.

SERVING SUGGESTION:

Add fresh herbs and serve with fresh fruit.

Nutrient Analysis: PER SERVING: 372 cal (1558kJ); Protein 17g; Total Fat 20g; Saturated Fat 5g; Carbohydrate 25g; Total Sugars 7g; Fiber 13g; Sodium 428mg; Potassium 589mg; Calcium 302mg; Iron 3.6mg; Zinc 2.0mg

TIP: Place leftover scrambled tofu in the refrigerator. Heat and serve on whole wheat toast for breakfast in the morning.

SERVING SUGGESTION: *Serve with your choice of beans and arugula/rocket salad.*

GF 🕐 Corn and Pea Fritters

Preparation time: 15 minutes **Cooking time:** 40 minutes **Serves:** 6-8

2 tablespoons water
1 onion, finely diced
3 tablespoons egg replacer
½ cup water
2¼ cups rice or soy milk
fortified with calcium/B12
2 cups plain whole wheat flour
or gluten-free flour, sifted
1 tablespoon aluminium-free baking powder
1 teaspoon salt (optional)
1 cup corn kernels
2 cups whole peas
⅛ teaspoon chili powder (optional)
⅓ cup chopped fresh mint
2 tablespoons lime zest
1 lime, juiced (optional)
2 tablespoons oil (for frying)

1. Heat water in a small pan and sauté onion until transparent.

2. In a separate bowl, whisk together egg replacer and water.

3. Add rice or soy milk, flour and baking powder and salt (optional) to the egg replacer mixture, and whisk until smooth.

4. Add corn kernels, peas, chili powder, mint, lime zest and lime juice, then stir until well combined.

5. Heat oil in frying pan, then place ¼ cup of batter into heated pan. Cook for about 4-5 minutes on each side. Place on a tray and put in the oven at low heat to keep warm until ready to serve. Repeat until all batter is used.

Nutrient Analysis: PER SERVING: 265 cal (1106kJ); Protein 10g; Total Fat 7g; Saturated Fat 1g; Carbohydrate 38g; Total Sugars 4g; Fiber 8g; Sodium 449mg; Potassium 598mg; Calcium 203mg; Iron 2.4mg; Zinc 1.3mg

Tortilla Cups with Beans and Salad

Preparation time: 20 minutes **Cooking time:** 30 minutes **Makes:** 30 cups

1 package whole wheat tortillas
1 onion, finely diced
¼ cup water
15.5 oz/420g can (no-added-salt, if available) chili beans
1-2 tablespoons Cashew Cream (see page 146)
or 1-2 tablespoons water
2 large lettuce leaves, finely shredded
2 tomatoes, finely diced
1 cob of fresh corn cooked and kernels cut off
1 small cucumber, finely diced
½ avocado, finely diced

1. Preheat oven to 325°F/165°C.

2. Using a round or fluted cookie cutter, cut 5 rounds out of the tortilla sheets. Press rounds into muffin tins and bake in the oven for 10 minutes or until slightly brown. Remove from oven, take out of trays and set aside to cool. They will become crisp as they cool.

3. Sauté onion with water in skillet or frying pan until soft.

4. Add beans and mash with potato masher, then add cashew cream or water if too thick.

5. Spoon prepared beans into tortilla cups.

6. Top beans with shredded lettuce, tomato, cucumber, corn and avocado.

TIP:

These are great served at a dinner party, or as a finger food for that special celebration.

Nutrient Analysis: PER CUP: 45 cal (190kJ); Protein 2g; Total Fat 2g; Saturated Fat <1g; Carbohydrate 4g; Total Sugars 1g; Fiber 2g; Sodium 57mg; Potassium 113mg; Calcium 13mg

SERVING SUGGESTION: *Serve with a mixed green salad sprinkled with nuts.*

CREATE YOUR OWN HEALTHY PIZZA

Crust options:
› Quick Pizza Crust recipe
› Whole wheat flat bread

Sauce alternatives:
› Tomato and Basil Sauce (see page 147)
› No-added-salt tomato paste
› Mild tomato salsa
› Hummus

Topping options:
› Artichoke
› Bell pepper/capsicum
› Olives
› Pineapple
› Baby spinach
› Red onion
› Beets/beetroot
› Roast pumpkin
› Mushrooms
› Arugula/rocket

Cheese alternatives:
› Savory Cashew Cream (see page 146)
› Cashew Cheese (see page 153)

Quick Pizza Crust

Preparation time: 15-20 minutes **Cooking time:** 20 minutes **Serves:** 6

Whole Wheat Crust

1 cup whole wheat flour
½ cup all-purpose flour
½ cup arrowroot powder
½ teaspoon salt (optional)
1 teaspoon egg replacer
½ tablespoon aluminium-free baking powder
1 tablespoon oil
¾ cup water

VARIATION:

For a gluten-free crust, replace the whole wheat flour and plain flour with 1½ cups of gluten-free flour of your choice.

Nutrient Analysis: PER SERVING: 190 cal (793kJ); Protein 4g; Total Fat 4g; Saturated Fat <1g; Carbohydrate 24g; Total Sugars <1g; Fiber3g; Sodium 433mg; Potassium 209mg; Calcium 63mg; Iron 1.0mg

1. Preheat oven to 350°F/180°C.

2. Sift flours, arrowroot, salt (optional), egg replacer and baking powder together in a large mixing bowl.

3. Mix oil and water together in a small sealed container and shake to combine. Pour into flour mixture and stir until well combined.

4. Knead the dough into a ball, adding more water if required. Mix should feel similar to pastry dough.

5. Lightly flour pizza pan/tray and place dough on tray. Using a floured rolling pin, roll the dough until it covers the pan/tray evenly.

6. Place pan/tray in oven for 8 minutes and continue with preparation of the toppings.

7. Allow pizza crust to cool slightly, then top with your favorite toppings.

8. Bake pizza 15-20 more minutes until toppings are cooked and pizza is evenly browned.

Main Meals

Tempting, tasty, terrific—so many hearty delights to discover and enjoy.

"So it's no longer a secret: one personal choice seems to influence long-term health prospects more than any other: what we eat."

[Dr Hans Diehl]

Eat More

GF ⏱ Lentil and Sesame Rissoles

Preparation time: 45 minutes **Cooking time:** 20 minutes **Serves:** 6

4 cups cooked brown lentils
¼ cup water or 1 teaspoon oil
1 small onion, finely chopped
4 cloves garlic, crushed
4 cups diced mushrooms
1½ tablespoons chopped
fresh thyme
2 tomatoes, finely chopped
⅓ cup walnuts, finely chopped
4 tablespoons no-added-
salt tomato paste
1 carrot, finely grated
2 teaspoons curry powder
3 teaspoons ground cumin
1 tablespoon low-sodium
soy sauce (GF) (optional)
1½ cups dried bread or
rice crumbs
½ cup sesame seeds

1. Preheat oven to 350°F/180°C.

2. Sauté onion and garlic in water until soft and slightly brown, then add the diced mushrooms and cook until mushrooms start to brown.

3. In a large bowl, combine cooked lentils, onion, garlic, mushrooms and thyme. Add tomatoes, walnuts, tomato paste, carrot, curry powder, cumin and soy sauce and mix well. Add 1 cup of bread/rice crumbs and combine.

4. Combine remaining bread/rice crumbs with sesame seeds in a separate bowl.

5. Divide mixture into ¼ cup-sized balls, flatten and coat in breadcrumb mixture.

6. Line a baking sheet/tray with baking paper/parchment or spray baking sheet with non-stick cooking spray. Place patties on tray and bake with broil/grill element on for approximately 6 minutes on each side. Turn broil/grill element off and bake in oven for a further 5-8 minutes.

TIP:

To prepare dry lentils ready for use, see table on page 18 and 19 as a guide.

Nutrient Analysis:
PER SERVING: 378 cal (1578kJ); Protein 20g; Total Fat 13g; Saturated Fat 2g; Carbohydrate 39g; Total Sugars 7g; Fiber 11g; Sodium 367mg; Potassium 897mg; Calcium 93mg; Iron 5.6mg; Zinc 2.9mg

Recipe kindly provided by Toowoomba CHIP Chapter, Queensland, Australia.

SERVING SUGGESTION: *Serve on a whole grain burger bun with fresh salad to create a healthy burger option.*

SERVING SUGGESTION: *Serve with a whole grain bread roll or a green salad.*

GF ◐ Mushroom and Lentil Stew

Preparation time: 15 minutes **Cooking time:** 15 minutes **Serves:** 6

1 onion, finely diced
2 cloves garlic, crushed
1 tablespoon oil
3 cups mushrooms, sliced
1 tablespoon no-added-salt tomato paste
2 x 14.5 oz/400g cans chopped tomatoes
2 x 15 oz cans brown lentils, drained and
rinsed or 3½ cups cooked brown lentils
1 tablespoon low-sodium tamari
sauce or soy sauce (GF)
1 teaspoon salt (optional)
½ cup Savory Cashew Cream (see page 146)
¼ cup parsley, chopped

1. Sauté onions and garlic in oil until lightly browned

2. Add mushrooms and cook until brown. Add tomato paste, stir through and cook for a further 2 minutes.

3. Add chopped tomatoes, lentils, tamari and salt (optional). Bring to a boil, turn heat down to simmer and cook for 5 minutes.

4. Add Savory Cashew Cream and stir well to combine. Stir in parsley just before serving.

TIP:

Make Savory Cashew Cream the day before to save time.

Nutrient Analysis: PER SERVING: 198 cal (829kJ); Protein 10g; Total Fat 9g; Saturated Fat 2g; Carbohydrate 15g; Total Sugars 6g; Fiber 7g; Sodium 492mg; Potassium 707mg; Calcium 59mg; Iron 3.5mg; Zinc 2.0mg

Complete Health Improvement Program – **EAT MORE** | 123

Black Bean Stew

Preparation time: 20 minutes **Cooking time:** 40 minutes **Serves:** 4-6

½ **medium onion, diced**
1 **medium sweet potato, peeled and diced**
3 **cups water**
2 x 15 oz/400g **cans black beans,
rinsed and drained**
14.5 oz/400g **can diced tomatoes**
⅔ **cup uncooked pearl barley**
1½ **teaspoon cumin powder**
½ **teaspoon salt (optional)**
1 **teaspoon chili powder (optional)**
½ **cup chopped fresh cilantro/coriander**
½ **lime, juiced**

1. Steam onion and sweet potato in soup pot with ½ cup water for about 5 minutes. Add remaining water, beans, tomatoes, barley, cumin, salt (optional) and chili powder (optional).

2. Bring to a boil, then reduce to a simmer for 20-30 minutes, until barley and sweet potato are cooked.

3. Add cilantro and lime juice and stir through.

4. Top with additional fresh cilantro to serve, if desired.

TIP:

If using dried beans, soak beans overnight, then cook for 1½-2 hours hours until tender.

Nutrient Analysis: PER SERVING: 207 cal (864kJ); Protein 11g; Total Fat 1g; Saturated Fat <1g; Carbohydrate 31g; Total Sugars 6g; Fiber 12g; Sodium 294mg; Potassium 633mg; Calcium 65mg; Iron 3.2mg; Zinc 1.8mg

Recipe kindly provided by the Itasca CHIP Chapter, Minnesota, USA.

SERVING SUGGESTION:
Serve with brown rice, whole grain bread roll or Corn Bread (see right).

Corn Bread

Preparation time: 15 minutes
Cooking time: 40 minutes **Makes:** 8

1¼ cups whole grain cornmeal/polenta
1 cup boiling water
¾ cup low-fat soy milk fortified with calcium/B12
1 tablespoon lemon juice
1 tablespoon oil
⅔ cup apple sauce (unsweetened)
½ teaspoon salt

1. Preheat oven to 350°F/180°C. Pour 1 cup boiling water over cornmeal in a heat-proof bowl. Cover and let stand for 10 minutes.

2. Combine soy milk and lemon juice together, and let stand for 1 minute.

3. Add oil, apple sauce and salt to milk mixture, then mix with the soaked cornmeal. Add dry cornmeal and combine.

4. Pour into ⅓ cup muffin tins and bake for 35–40 minutes.

Nutrient Analysis: PER SERVING: 120 cal (502kJ); Protein 3g; Total Fat 3g; Saturated Fat <1g; Carbohydrate 20g; Total Sugars 5g; Fiber 1g; Sodium 162mg; Potassium 88mg; Calcium 35mg

Recipe kindly provided by Hinsdale CHIP Chapter, Illinois, USA.

GF 🕐 *Garbanzo and Eggplant Stew*

Preparation time: 20 minutes **Cooking time:** 1 hour 10 minutes **Serves:** 4

1 large eggplant/aubergine, cubed
oil spray
1 tablespoon oil
1 large onion, chopped
1½ cups water
1 teaspoon cumin, or more to taste
1 large potato, cubed
2 x 15 oz/400g cans garbanzos/
chickpeas, rinsed and drained
3 fresh tomatoes, diced
½ teaspoon salt (optional)

1. Preheat oven to 400°F/210°C. Place eggplant onto a baking sheet/tray and spray lightly with oil. Place in the oven to bake for 25 minutes or until lightly browned.

2. In a medium saucepan, add oil and sauté onions until transparent. Add ½ cup of water, cover and continue cooking for about 2 minutes. Set mixture aside.

3. In another medium saucepan, add 1 cup of water and cumin. Bring to a boil. Add potato and lower heat to simmer.

4. Cook for about 5 minutes, then add garbanzo, eggplant, tomatoes and cooked onion. An additional 1 cup of water can be added at this time, if needed.

5. Add seasoning to desired taste. Cook on low heat for about 15 minutes, stirring occasionally, until potato and eggplant are cooked.

TIP:

Add some additional flavor with a teaspoon of curry powder, extra cumin or some freshly chopped parsley.

Nutrient Analysis: PER SERVING: 241 cal (1009kJ); Protein 11g; Total Fat 5g; Saturated Fat <1g; Carbohydrate 31g; Total Sugars 7g; Fiber 10g; Sodium 543mg; Potassium 835mg; Calcium 91mg; Iron 3.2mg; Zinc 1.8mg

GF *Lentil Shepherd's Pie*

Preparation time: 15 minutes **Cooking time:** 60 minutes **Serves:** 6

2 lb/1kg potatoes, peeled and diced
1 tablespoon oil
1 medium onion, chopped
1 stalk celery, finely chopped
1 large carrot, finely chopped
1 teaspoon curry powder
1 lb/500g jar low-sodium tomato-based pasta sauce
2 x 15 oz/400g cans brown lentils, drained and rinsed or 3½ cups cooked brown lentils
1 cup frozen peas
1 tablespoon almond butter
½ cup soy or rice milk fortified with calcium/B12

1. Preheat oven to 350°F/180°. Place potatoes in a large saucepan and cover with hot water. Bring to a boil, then reduce heat and simmer until tender.

2. Heat oil in a medium pot and sauté onion, celery and carrot until soft.

3. Add curry powder and sauté for 1 minute.

4. Add pasta sauce, lentils and peas, and bring to a boil. Reduce heat and simmer for 5 minutes.

5. Drain potatoes, and add almond butter and soy milk. Mash until smooth.

6. Spoon lentil mixture into one large oven-proof dish or 6 one-cup small oven-proof dishes. Top with mashed potato.

7. Bake in a moderate oven for 40 minutes.

Nutrient Analysis: PER SERVING: 303 cal (1136kJ); Protein 13g; Total Fat 6g; Saturated Fat <1g; Carbohydrate 36g; Total Sugars 8g; Fiber 8g; Sodium 84mg; Potassium 1055mg; Calcium 64mg; Iron 2.9mg; Zinc 1.8mg

SERVING SUGGESTION: *Serve with a fresh salad or a variety of steamed vegetables on the side.*

SERVING SUGGESTION: *Serve with cooked medium-grain brown rice.*

GF ⏱ *Pumpkin and Garbanzo Satay*

Preparation time: 25 minutes **Cooking time:** 25 minutes **Serves:** 4

¼ **cup water**
1 **onion, chopped**
2 **garlic cloves, crushed**
2 **teaspoons grated fresh ginger**
1 **long red chili pepper, seeds and membrane**
removed, finely chopped (optional)
1.5 **lb/700g pumpkin or butternut squash, peeled,**
chopped into chunks
1 **cup reduced-fat coconut milk**
½ **cup low-sodium liquid vegetable broth/stock (GF)**
2 **cups cauliflower florets**
⅓ **cup crunchy natural peanut butter**
(no-added-salt or sugar)
1 **tablespoon low-sodium soy sauce (GF)**
2 **teaspoons honey**
15 **oz/400g can garbanzos/**
chickpeas, rinsed and drained
¼ **cup chopped fresh cilantro/coriander**
2 **oz/60g baby spinach leaves**

1. Heat water in a large saucepan, then add onion and cook for 4-5 minutes until soft. Add garlic, ginger and chili and cook for 1 more minute, stirring occasionally.

2. Add pumpkin and stir to combine. Pour in coconut milk and stock, and bring to a boil. Cover and reduce heat to simmer for 8-10 minutes until pumpkin is just cooked.

3. Add cauliflower, cover and cook for 3-4 minutes until cauliflower is tender. Add peanut butter, soy sauce, honey and garbanzos. Stir to combine and heat through. Stir in cilantro and baby spinach leaves.

Nutrient Analysis: PER SERVING: 386 cal (1612kJ); Protein 16g; Total Fat 19g; Saturated Fat 6g; Carbohydrate 31g; Total Sugars 17g; Fiber 10g; Sodium 434mg; Potassium 1305mg; Calcium 101mg; Iron 3.4mg; Zinc 2.1mg

Complete Health Improvement Program – **EAT MORE** | 131

Pastry Crust

1½ cups whole wheat flour
½ cup almond butter
⅓ cup oil
⅓ cup water
2½ teaspoons baking powder
pinch of salt (optional)

1. Preheat oven to 350˚F/180ºC. Mix together flour, baking powder and salt, and rub almond butter through using fingers. Add oil and water, then mix to form a dough.

2. Press dough into pie tin, and spread out evenly to cover the bottom and sides of the tin. Place baking paper over the top and cover with uncooked rice to keep baking paper in place. Place in oven and bake for 5 minutes.

Roast Vegetable Quiche

Preparation time: 40 minutes **Cooking time:** 50 minutes **Serves:** 12

Roast Vegetables

½ medium eggplant/aubergine, diced
1 medium sweet potato, peeled and diced
1 medium zucchini, diced
1 onion, diced
½ red bell pepper/capsicum, diced
1 tablespoon fresh basil, chopped
2 tablespoons fresh parsley, chopped

Filling

½ cup egg replacer
2 cups rice or soy milk fortified with calcium/B12
½ teaspoon garlic powder
½ teaspoon onion powder
½ teaspoon salt (optional)
¼ teaspoon ground turmeric

Roast Vegetables

1. Preheat oven to 475ºF/240ºC. Place vegetables, except onion and bell pepper, in a single layer on a baking sheet/tray. Bake in oven for 15 minutes until browned.

2. Fry onion separately in a pan with a small amount of water until browned.

3. Combine roast vegetables, bell pepper and onion and place a single layer of vegetables over the pastry. Sprinkle chopped basil and parsley evenly over the vegetables.

Filling

1. Whisk egg replacer, rice milk, garlic powder, onion powder, salt (optional) and turmeric until well combined.

2. Pour evenly over vegetables in the pie tin, and bake in the oven for 30 minutes until set.

Nutrient Analysis: PER SERVING: 257 cal (1075kJ); Protein 7g; Total Fat 14g; Saturated Fat 2g; Carbohydrate 24g; Total Sugars 3g; Fiber 3g; Sodium 350mg; Potassium 250mg; Calcium 70mg; Iron 1.0mg

TIP: Refrigerate the leftovers and have for lunch or dinner the next day. Roast Vegetable Quiche tastes great straight from the fridge or warmed up.

SERVING SUGGESTION: *Serve over steamed rice and garnish with cilantro.*

GF 🕐 *Red Lentil and Vegetable Dahl*

Preparation time: 20 minutes **Cooking time:** 50 minutes **Serves:** 6

1 medium onion, finely diced
3 cloves of garlic, minced
½ cup water
2 teaspoons grated fresh ginger
2 teaspoons ground cumin
2 teaspoons ground cilantro/coriander
1 teaspoon turmeric
¼ teaspoon chili powder (optional)
2 cups dry red lentils, rinsed
2 tablespoons no-added-salt tomato paste
2 whole tomatoes, diced
5 cups water
2 teaspoons curry powder/garam masala
1½ teaspoons salt (optional)
¼ cup fresh cilantro/coriander (garnish)

1. Sauté onion and garlic with ½ cup of water, in a medium saucepan, until transparent.

2. Add ginger, cumin, cilantro/coriander, turmeric and chili powder, and cook for a further 3-4 minutes watching that it does not stick to saucepan. Add more water, if needed.

3. Add lentils, tomato paste, tomatoes and 5 cups of water. Bring to a boil with lid on and reduce to simmer for 15-20 minutes or until lentils are cooked.

4. Add curry powder and simmer for 5 more minutes.

5. Add salt or alternative seasoning and garnish with cilantro/coriander.

TIP:

Add steamed/blanched cauliflower, frozen peas, roast eggplant, roast pumpkin, roast sweet potato or any other vegetables of your choice to make a complete meal.

Nutrient Analysis: PER SERVING: 214 cal (895kJ); Protein 17g; Total Fat 2g; Saturated Fat <1g; Carbohydrate 28g; Total Sugars 4g; Fiber 11g; Sodium 609mg; Potassium 792mg; Calcium 78mg; Iron 6.0mg; Zinc 2.3mg

Complete Health Improvement Program – **EAT MORE** | 135

GF ⏱ *Nutty Potato Bites*

Preparation time: 20 minutes **Cooking time:** 45 minutes **Serves:** 7

¼ **cup water**
2 **onions, finely chopped**
2 **cloves garlic, crushed**
3-4 **medium potatoes, peeled and grated**
1 **cup walnuts, ground**
1 **cup dry whole wheat bread crumbs or rice crumbs**
1 **teaspoon sage or 2 teaspoons dried Italian herbs**
2 **tablespoons nutritional yeast flakes**
1 **tablespoon whole wheat flour,**
besan flour or soy flour
¼ **teaspoon salt (optional)**
2 **tablespoons no-added-salt tomato paste**

Recipe kindly provided by Toowoomba CHIP Chapter, Queensland, Australia.

1. Preheat oven to 350°F/180°C.

2. Sauté onion and garlic with water in a skillet or frying pan until soft.

3. In a large bowl, combine potatoes, walnuts, bread/rice crumbs, herbs, yeast flakes, flour, salt (optional) and tomato paste. Mix well and form into balls using a tablespoon of mixture for each.

4. Place on a baking sheet/tray and bake for 40-45 minutes.

Nutrient Analysis: PER SERVING: 204 cal (852kJ); Protein 6g; Total Fat 9g; Saturated Fat <1g; Carbohydrate 22g; Total Sugars 3g; Fiber 4g; Sodium 216mg; Potassium 466mg; Calcium 39mg; Iron 1.4mg

TIP: Great served as a starter or as finger food for a special occasion.

White Sauce

¾ cup all-purpose
  or whole wheat flour
4 cups rice milk fortified
  with calcium/B12
1 teaspoon salt (optional)
1 tablespoon nutritional
  yeast flakes (optional)

1. Combine flour with 1 cup of the rice milk in a container with a tight-fitting lid. Shake until all lumps disappear.

2. Heat remaining 3 cups of rice milk until it comes to a boil, add flour mixture and whisk to combine. Reduce heat and allow sauce to cook through for 3-5 more minutes, stirring occasionally.

3. Add salt and yeast flakes (optional), and stir through.

TIP: *Try baking Roast Vegetable and Lentil Lasagna ahead of time and freeze for use at a later date.*

Roast Vegetable and Lentil Lasagna

Preparation time: 40 minutes **Cooking time:** 1 hour 10 minutes **Serves:** 8

Roast Vegetables

2 medium eggplant/aubergines,
  cut into ½-inch/1.5-
  centimeter slices
olive oil spray (optional)
4 medium red bell peppers/
  capsicum
9 oz/250g package whole wheat
  or gluten-free lasagna
  noodles/sheets
½ cup pine nuts

Tomato Sauce

3 tablespoons water
1 medium onion, finely diced
3 cloves of garlic, minced
2 x 14.5 oz/400g cans chopped
  or crushed tomatoes
1 bay leaf
1 tablespoon honey (optional)
½ teaspoon salt (optional)
20 leaves fresh basil, chopped
1 cup cooked brown lentils

Roast Vegetables

1. Preheat oven to 400°F/210°C. Place eggplant on a baking sheet/tray in a single layer and lightly spray with oil. Bake for 20 minutes until browned and tender.

2. Cut bell peppers in half, remove seeds, and place face down on a baking sheet/tray. Roast until blackened and sunken. Remove from oven and place in a bowl, cover with plastic wrap and leave to cool. Once cooled, remove skin and cut in quarters.

3. Make Tomato Sauce and White Sauce while vegetables are roasting.

Tomato Sauce

1. Heat water in a saucepan. Add onion and garlic, and sauté for 3-5 minutes until onion is transparent.

2. Add tomatoes and bay leaf, and cook for 3-5 more minutes. Add honey and salt (optional).

3. Remove from heat and blend with a stick blender or use blender. Hold lid firmly in place while processing hot liquids.

4. Add basil and cooked lentils, and stir through.

SERVING SUGGESTION: *Serve with mixed arugula/rocket and baby spinach.*

To Assemble

1. Preheat oven to 375°F/190°C. Cover the bottom of an 8 x 11-inch/20 x 30-centimeter lasagna dish with a thin layer of tomato sauce. Place lasagna noodles/sheets on top, then spread over one-third of the tomato sauce.

2. Layer with eggplant, white sauce and half the bell peppers, then sprinkle with one-third of pine nuts. Repeat layers, finishing with white sauce, and sprinkle with pine nuts on top.

3. Bake for 45 minutes or until browned and lasagna sheets are cooked through.

Nutrient Analysis: PER SERVING: 399 cal (1670kJ); Protein 12g; Total Fat 11g; Saturated Fat <1g; Carbohydrate 59g; Total Sugars 17g; Fiber 9g; Sodium 658mg; Potassium 562mg; Calcium 205mg; Iron 1.9mg; Zinc 1.3mg

Pesto

1 bunch fresh basil
2 cloves garlic
⅓ cup pine nuts
1 tablespoon sesame seeds
3 tablespoons water
2 teaspoons oil
½ teaspoon salt (optional)
¼ cup walnuts

1. Place all ingredients in food processor and mix until well combined.

2. Place pesto mix into a small bowl, drizzle with a small amount of olive oil, and cover with plastic wrap, so the plastic is touching the pesto, to keep out as much air as possible. Place in refrigerator to cool.

TIP: *Great served as a starter or appetizer when entertaining.*

Pumpkin Risotto Bites

Preparation time: 25 minutes **Cooking time:** 1 hour **Serves:** 10

Risotto

¼ cup water
3 cloves garlic, minced
1 onion, diced
1 lb/500g pumpkin or butternut squash, diced in 0.5-inch/1-centimeter cubes
1½ cup medium-grain brown rice
3 tablespoons low-sodium vegetable broth/stock powder (GF)
4 cups boiling water
¼ cup parsley, chopped
1 teaspoon salt (optional)
⅓ cup dry breadcrumbs or rice crumbs
pine nuts to garnish

Nutrient Analysis: PER SERVING: 140 cal (587kJ); Protein 4g; Total Fat 9g; Saturated Fat <1g; Carbohydrate 10g; Total Sugars 4g; Fiber 3g; Sodium 402mg; Potassium 355mg; Calcium 59mg; Iron 1.1mg

1. Heat water in a large saucepan. Add garlic and onion, and sauté until transparent.

2. Add pumpkin to onion and garlic, and cook for 2 more minutes.

3. Add rice and continue to cook for 5 more minutes until rice becomes transparent.

4. Add stock powder and water, and return to a boil. Reduce heat and simmer until water is absorbed. Stir regularly to ensure rice does not stick to the bottom of the saucepan. Check to see if rice is cooked. Add more water as required.

5. When ready, add chopped parsley, salt (optional) and bread/rice crumbs, and stir through. Set aside to cool.

6. Form into balls, using a 1 tablespoon measure and refrigerate.

To Assemble

1. When cool, remove risotto balls from fridge and place ½ teaspoon of pesto on top of each ball to garnish. Sprinkle with chopped pine nuts to serve.

White Sauce

1 cup light coconut milk
¾ cup plain whole wheat flour
3 cups rice milk fortified with
   calcium/B12
1 teaspoons salt (optional)
½ teaspoon turmeric

1. Combine flour with coconut milk and whisk until smooth.

2. Heat rice milk until it comes to a boil. Add flour mixture and whisk to combine. Reduce heat and allow sauce to cook through for a further 3-5 minutes, stirring occasionally.

3. Add salt and turmeric, and stir through.

Nutrient Analysis: PER SERVING: 336 cal (1403kJ); Protein 10g; Total Fat 5g; Saturated Fat 2g; Carbohydrate 59g; Total Sugars 19g; Fiber 7g; Sodium 641mg; Potassium 808mg; Calcium 176mg; Iron 1.5mg

Pumpkin and Spinach Lasagna

Preparation time: 40 minutes **Cooking time:** 1 hour 10 minutes **Serves:** 8

Pumpkin and Spinach

2 lb/1kg pumpkin or butternut
squash, cut into ½-inch/
1.5-centimeter slices
olive oil spray
1 small bunch fresh
spinach, shredded
9 oz/250g package whole wheat
or gluten-free lasagna
noodles/sheets

Tomato Sauce

3 tablespoons water
1 medium onion, finely diced
3 cloves of garlic, minced
2 x 14.5 oz/400g cans chopped
or crushed tomatoes
1 bay leaf
1 tablespoon honey (optional)
½ teaspoon salt (optional)
10 leaves fresh basil, chopped

Pumpkin and Spinach

1. Preheat oven to 375°F/190°C. Place pumpkin on a baking tray in a single layer and spray lightly with oil. Bake for 15 minutes or until browned and tender.

2. Make Tomato Sauce and White Sauce while vegetables are roasting.

Tomato Sauce

1. Heat water in a saucepan. Add onion and garlic, and sauté for 3-5 minutes until onion is clear.

2. Add tomatoes and bay leaf, and cook for 3-5 more minutes.

3. Add honey and salt (optional).

4. Remove from heat and blend with a stick blender or in blender. Hold lid firmly in place while processing hot liquids.

5. Add basil and stir through.

To Assemble

1. To assemble, use a standard baking pan size (8 X 11 inches/20 x 28 centimeters), cover the base with a thin layer of Tomato Sauce. Place lasagna noodles/sheets on top, then spread one-third of the Tomato Sauce on top. Layer with pumpkin, spinach leaves and cover with a thin layer of White Sauce.

2. Repeat layers twice, finishing with White Sauce.

3. Place in the oven to bake for 45 minutes or until browned on top and lasagna noodles/sheets are cooked through.

OPTIONS:

Use a sandwich press to cook pumpkin: Place pumpkin slices on hotplate, lower lid and cook for 10 minutes or until browned and tender.

Tomato Sauce: Use a jar of purchased tomato-based sauce.

Gluten-free option: Use gluten-free lasagna noodles/sheets and gluten-free flour in the white sauce.

VARIATIONS:

Add lentils, cannellini beans, kidney beans or vegetarian mince to tomato sauce.

Add additional vegetables, such as roast bell pepper/capsicum, mushrooms, eggplant or zucchini.

Complete Health Improvement Program – **EAT MORE** | 143

"Embrace healthy eating habits with whole foods, fruits, veggies, whole grains and legumes. You will be able to eat more and feel satisfied. An even more important bonus is marked improvement in your health."

[Andrea Avery MD]

Spreads and Dips

Add some excitement to your day with these vibrant dips and delicious sauces.
Great for adding a little pizzazz to any occasion.

"With CHIP, you can eat all you want of nature's whole plant foods and feel full; you'll have excellent nutrition and yet you don't have to worry about the calories."

[Dr Hans Diehl]

Eat More

Eggless Mayonnaise GF

Preparation time: 10 minutes
Makes: 2 cups

- 6 teaspoons water
- 3 tablespoons egg replacer
- ½ cup oil
- 1 teaspoon lemon juice
- ½ teaspoon salt (optional)
- 2 teaspoons honey
- 2 teaspoons whole mustard seeds

1. Process water and egg replacer in food processor, then slowly drizzle in oil until the mixture is well combined and thickened. Add remaining ingredients and mix until well combined.

Nutrient Analysis: PER ¼ CUP SERVING: 92 cal (385kJ); Protein <1g; Total Fat 9g; Saturated Fat 2g; Carbohydrate 3g; Total Sugars 1g; Fiber <1g; Sodium 99mg; Potassium 1mg; Calcium <1mg

 Rating for all three recipes.

Creamy Cashew White Sauce GF

Preparation time: 10 minutes
Makes: 1 cup

- 1 cup hot water
- ½ cup raw cashews
- 1 teaspoon low-sodium broth/stock powder of your choice
- ¼ teaspoon salt (optional)

1. Place all ingredients in a blender and process on high until mixture becomes smooth. Hold lid firmly in place while processing hot liquids.

2. Pour into a saucepan and bring to a boil, stirring constantly until thickened.

3. Remove from heat and serve hot.

TIP: *Serve over broccoli and other green vegetables.*

Nutrient Analysis: PER ¼ CUP SERVING: 110 cal (460kJ); Protein 3g; Total Fat 9g; Saturated Fat 2g; Carbohydrate 3g; Total Sugars 1g; Fiber 1g; Sodium 244mg; Potassium 103mg; Calcium 7mg; Zinc 1.0mg

Savory Cashew Cream GF

Preparation time: 10 minutes
Makes: ¾ cup

- 1 cup raw cashews
- ¾ cup water
- ½ teaspoon salt (optional)

1. Place cashews, water and salt (optional) in blender, and blend until very smooth consistency.

DID YOU KNOW? *Studies have shown that eating a small handful of nuts five or more times per week can reduce the risk of heart disease by about 50 per cent.*

Nutrient Analysis: PER ¼ CUP SERVING: 288 cal (1202kJ); Protein 8g; Total Fat 24g; Saturated Fat 4g; Carbohydrate 8g; Total Sugars 3g; Fiber 3g; Sodium 401mg; Potassium 272mg; Calcium 18mg; Iron 2.5mg, Zinc 2.7mg

Recipe kindly provided by Clark County CHIP Chapter, Washington, USA.

TIP:
This is a great dipping sauce for the Nutty Potato Bites (see page 136), can be used as a base for a pasta sauce, or in place of tomato ketchup/sauce.

Tomato and Basil Sauce

Preparation time: 5 minutes
Cooking time: 10 minutes **Serves:** 6-8

3 tablespoons water or 1 tablespoon oil
1 medium onion, finely diced
3 cloves of garlic, crushed
2 x 14.5 oz/400g cans chopped or crushed tomatoes
1 bay leaf
1 tablespoon honey (optional)
½ teaspoon salt (optional)
10 leaves fresh basil, shredded finely

1. Heat water or oil in a medium saucepan. Add onion and garlic, and sauté for 3-5 minutes until onion is transparent.

2. Add tomatoes and bay leaf, and cook for 3-5 more minutes.

3. Add honey and salt (optional), and stir through.

4. Take sauce off the stove, remove bay leaf and blend with a stick blender or in blender. Hold lid firmly in place while processing hot liquids.

5. Add basil and stir through.

Nutrient Analysis: PER SERVING: 40 cal (168kJ); Protein 1g; Total Fat <1g; Saturated Fat <1g; Carbohydrate 7g; Total Sugars 7g; Fiber 2g; Sodium 276mg; Potassium 231mg; Calcium 31mg

SERVING SUGGESTION: *Serve warm or cold as a spread on whole grain toast, pancakes, waffles or biscuits/scones.*

Date, Apricot and Ginger Jam

Preparation time: 15 minutes
Makes: 2¼ cups

2 cups dried dates
1 cup dried apricots
⅓ cup uncrystallized ginger
2 cups hot water

1. Soak dates, apricots and ginger in hot water for 10 minutes.

2. Place in food processor and blend until smooth.

Nutrient Analysis: PER SERVING: 52 cal (219kJ); Protein <1g; Total Fat <1g; Saturated Fat <1g; Carbohydrate 12g; Total Sugars 12g; Fiber 2g; Sodium 4mg; Potassium 164mg; Calcium 9mg

Sweet Cashew Cream

Preparation time: 10 minutes
Makes: 2½ cups

2 cups raw cashews
1½ cups water
2 tablespoons honey
1½ teaspoons vanilla extract

1. Mix all ingredients together in a blender and process until smooth.

2. Add more water for pouring consistency.

TIP: *If making the day ahead, keep in the refrigerator overnight. You will need to add more water the next day as the cashews will absorb liquid.*

VARIATION: *For chocolate cashew cream, add 3 tablespoons raw cacao powder.*

Nutrient Analysis: PER ¼ CUP SERVING: 188 cal (784kJ); Protein 5g; Total Fat 14g; Saturated Fat 2g; Carbohydrate 10g; Total Sugars 6g; Fiber 2g; Sodium 4mg; Potassium 163mg; Calcium 11mg; Iron 1.5mg, Zinc 1.7mg

Beet and Bean Dip GF

Preparation time: 10 minutes
Makes: 1½ cups

1 medium beet/beetroot, peeled and steamed
1 teaspoon oil
3 teaspoons lemon juice
15 oz/400g can cannellini beans, drained and rinsed
¼ cup pine nuts
½ teaspoon salt (optional)
¼ cup water

1. Place all ingredients in a food processor and blend until well combined.

Nutrient Analysis: PER ¼ CUP SERVING: 141 cal (588kJ); Protein 5g; Total Fat 9g; Saturated Fat <1g; Carbohydrate 8g; Total Sugars 3g; Fiber 5g; Sodium 588mg; Potassium 247mg; Calcium 29mg; Iron 1.6mg; Zinc 1.0mg.

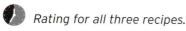

Rating for all three recipes.

Minted Pea Hummus GF

Preparation time: 10 minutes
Makes: 2 cups

1½ cups frozen baby peas, defrosted
1 large clove garlic (or 2 small)
15 oz/400g can garbanzos/chickpeas, drained and rinsed
1 tablespoon tahini
¼ cup lemon juice
¼ teaspoon salt (optional)
¼ cup fresh mint leaves

1. Steam peas and garlic for 2 minutes. Rinse in ice-cold water and drain.

2. Place all ingredients in a food processor and blend until smooth.

Nutrient Analysis: PER ¼ CUP SERVING: 72 cal (302kJ); Protein 4g; Total Fat 2g; Saturated Fat <1g; Carbohydrate 7g; Total Sugars 1g; Fiber 4g; Sodium 151mg; Potassium 101mg; Calcium 34mg; Iron 1.2mg; Zinc 1.0mg

Red Pepper and Lima Bean Dip GF

Preparation time: 35 minutes
Cooking time: 25 minutes **Makes:** 1 cup

1 red bell pepper/capsicum, deseeded and cut in half
15 oz/400g can lima/butter beans, drained and rinsed
1 teaspoon lemon juice
1 teaspoon salt (optional)
2-3 small cloves garlic

1. Preheat oven to 475°F/250°C. Place bell pepper face down on a lightly oiled oven tray and roast for 25 minutes or until blackened and sunken on top.

2. Remove peppers from oven, place in a bowl, cover in plastic wrap and leave to cool and sweat. When cooled, remove skin.

3. Place roasted peppers, lima beans, lemon juice, salt (optional) and garlic into a food processor, and mix until well combined with a smooth texture.

Nutrient Analysis: PER ¼ CUP SERVING: 28 cal (119kJ); Protein 2g; Total Fat <1g; Saturated Fat <1g; Carbohydrate 3g; Total Sugars 3g; Fiber 3g; Sodium 596mg; Potassium 184mg; Calcium 12mg

SERVING SUGGESTION: *Serve with pita bread, rice crackers, rice cakes or vegetable sticks.*

TIP:
Serve on whole grain toast, as a dip or in your favorite sandwich.

Hummus Dip

Preparation time: 10 minutes
Makes: 1½ cups

15 oz/400g can garbanzos/chickpeas, drained and rinsed
1 clove garlic
1 teaspoon lemon juice
¼ teaspoon salt (optional)
½ tablespoon tahini
¼ cup water

1. Place all ingredients into a food processor and blend until smooth.

Nutrient Analysis: PER ¼ CUP SERVING: 56 cal (232kJ); Protein 3g; Total Fat 2g; Saturated Fat <1g; Carbohydrate 6g; Total Sugars <1g; Fiber 2g; Sodium 196mg; Potassium 61mg; Calcium 23mg

Cashew Cheese GF

Preparation time: 10 minutes
Cooking time: 5 minutes **Makes:** 7-8 cups of grated cheese

2½ tablespoons agar agar powder
4 cups boiling water
1 red or yellow bell pepper/capsicum, deseeded
2 cups raw cashews
2½ tablespoons lemon juice
½ cup nutritional yeast flakes (optional)
1 teaspoon low-sodium soy sauce (GF)
2 teaspoons salt (optional)
1½ teaspoons onion powder
1½ teaspoons garlic powder

1. In a saucepan, whisk agar agar powder into boiling water, then boil 1-2 more minutes. Cool slightly.

2. Place bell peppers and remaining ingredients in blender with the boiled water and agar agar. Blend until very smooth for 1-2 minutes. Hold lid firmly in place while processing hot liquids.

3. Pour into containers to cool then cover and place in the refrigerator to set.

Nutrient Analysis: PER ¼ CUP SERVING: 61 cal (255kJ); Protein 2g; Total Fat 5g; Saturated Fat <1g; Carbohydrate 2g; Total Sugars <1g ; Fiber <1g; Sodium 156mg; Potassium 85mg; Calcium 7mg

Recipe kindly provided by Clark County CHIP Chapter, Washington, USA.

TIP: Slice or grate to use in place of cheese. Cashew Cheese can also be frozen to use at a later date.

Desserts

Nature's finest dessert: fresh fruit filled with life-giving nutrients.
But for those special occasions, choose from this delectable variety of desserts.
(Note: some desserts may be more calorie dense. Choose your servings wisely.)

*"It has been said, 'Life is short, eat dessert first.'
With these healthy treats, you can afford to!"*

[Dr Darren Morton]

Eat More

Crust

1½ cups whole wheat flour or gluten-free flour
½ cup almond butter
⅓ cup oil
⅓ cup warm water

1. Preheat oven to 350°F/180°C.

2. Spray the base of an 11-inch/28-centimeter springform pan lightly with oil.

3. Combine flour and almond butter with fingers.

4. Mix oil and water in a sealed container, shake to combine, then stir into flour mixture and form into a dough.

5. Wet counter top slightly, and place plastic wrap over a dampened flat surface. Place dough on plastic wrap and cover with another layer of plastic wrap.

6. Roll out dough ¼ inch thick. Remove the top layer of plastic wrap and place dough upside down into springform pan. Position dough into place using fingers, making sure pastry goes half way up the edges. Remove remaining plastic wrap.

7. Bake crust for 10 minutes before adding filling.

GF · Pumpkin and Spice Pie

Preparation time: 30 minutes **Cooking time:** 45 minutes **Serves:** 12

Filling

2 lb/800g pumpkin or 29 oz can pumpkin
2 cups dates
1½ teaspoons mixed spice/pumpkin pie spice
4 tablespoons cornstarch or arrowroot powder
1 cup light coconut milk
3 tablespoons honey

1. If using fresh pumpkin, chop pumpkin into small pieces and place in saucepan with dates. Cover with water and boil until pumpkin is soft. Strain cooked dates and pumpkin. Combine with spice, cornstarch, coconut milk and honey in blender. Then blend until smooth.

OR

If using canned pumpkin, soften the dates in hot water for a few minutes, then combine canned pumpkin, dates, spice, cornstarch, coconut milk and honey in blender. Then blend until smooth.

2. Pour mixture into partially baked crust and spread evenly over pastry. Place in oven and bake for 35 minutes.

3. Set aside to cool, then refrigerate until cold and set.

Majority of total sugars sourced from whole foods.

Nutrient Analysis: PER SERVING: 364 cal (1523kJ); Protein 7g; Total Fat 14g; Saturated Fat 1g; Carbohydrate 48g; Total Sugars 31g; Fiber 6g; Sodium 8mg; Potassium 548mg; Calcium 35mg; Iron 1.7mg

VARIATION: For a richer almond flavor, use almond extract instead of vanilla.

GF Almond Cranberry Cookies

Preparation time: 10 minutes **Cooking time:** 8 minutes **Makes:** 21 cookies

1 cup raw whole almonds
1 cup tapioca starch
1 tablespoon vanilla extract
¼ teaspoon salt (optional)
1 tablespoon lime zest
⅓ cup oil
¼ cup honey
¼ cup dry chopped cranberries

1. Preheat oven to 350°F/180° C.

2. Grind almonds in blender or food processor by pulsing until they reach a meal-like texture. Pass through a sieve if mixture contains big lumps. Re-pulse big lumps only if present.

3. Place all ingredients, except cranberries, in a food processor and blend until a smooth dough is formed.

4. Fold in the chopped cranberries using your hands.

5. Roll out dough ¼ inch thick and cut using a cookie cutter.

5. Bake in oven for 8 minutes or until golden brown.

TIP:

Do not over-grind the almonds or you will end up with almond butter.

Nutrient Analysis: PER COOKIE: 108 cal (450kJ); Protein 2g; Total Fat 7g; Saturated Fat 1g; Carbohydrate 11g; Total Sugars 5g; Fiber <1g; Sodium 31mg; Potassium 52mg

Avocado and Cashew Cream Parfait

Preparation time: 60 minutes **Refrigeration Time:** Overnight **Serves:** 12

Avocado Mousse
6 ripe avocados
1 cup lemon juice, freshly squeezed
1⅓ cups honey

1. Remove skin and seed from avocados, and place the green flesh into a food processor, removing all brown spots as you go. Add lemon juice and honey, and blend until smooth and creamy.

Chocolate Cashew Cream
2 tablespoons raw cacao powder
1 cup raw cashews
2 tablespoons honey
1⅓ cups water

1. Place cacao powder, cashew nuts, honey and water into blender, and blend until a smooth and creamy consistency.

Sugars are noted as being primarily sourced from refined sources, therefore should be consumed sparingly.

Crumble
1 cup raisins/sultanas
1 cup pecans
1 teaspoon tahini
¼ cup unsweetened shredded coconut

For decoration
18 oz/500g blueberries
6-8 strawberries, sliced
or 2-3 kiwi fruit, sliced

Crumble
1. Combine raisins/sultanas, pecans, tahini and coconut in food processor, and mix until well combined.

To Assemble
1. Place a layer of blueberries across the bottom of a parfait dish, and cover lightly with a thin layer of crumble mix.

2. Place sliced strawberries around the outside of the parfait dish to decorate. Pour about one-third of Chocolate Cashew Cream mixture over crumble. Be sure to fill all the gaps.

3. Top with one-third of the Avocado Mousse, then repeat layers of berries, crumble, Cashew Cream and Avocado Mousse. Cover lightly with crumble mixture and top with blueberries to finish.

4. Place in refrigerator to set, preferably overnight.

Nutrient Analysis: PER SERVING: 494 cal (2067kJ); Protein 6g; Total Fat 26g; Saturated Fat 5g; Carbohydrate 58g; Total Sugars 55g; Fiber 5g; Sodium 18mg; Potassium 679mg; Calcium 41mg; Iron 1.9mg; Zinc 2.7mg

NOTE: *This dessert should only be consumed for special occasions. Choose small servings.*

SERVING SUGGESTION: *Serve with fresh fruit, nuts and Sweet Cashew Cream (see page 149).*

GF ⏱ *Cornmeal Cake with Citrus Zest*

Preparation time: 20 minutes **Cooking time:** 10 minutes **Serves:** 12

2 cups rice milk fortified with calcium/B12
1 cup whole grain cornmeal/polenta
½ cup light coconut milk
½ cup chopped raw almonds
½ cup raisins/sultanas
¼ cup honey
1 tablespoon finely grated lemon zest
⅓ cup lemon juice
1½ teaspoons pumpkin pie spice/mixed spice
1 teaspoon vanilla extract

1. Bring rice milk to a boil in a medium saucepan. Stirring constantly with whisk, add cornmeal gradually in a thin stream. Reduce heat to medium and whisk for 5 minutes or until very thick.

2. Reduce heat to low and add remaining ingredients, stirring well after each addition.

3. Press into a 9-inch/23-centimeter round cake tin and smooth top.

4. Cool in the fridge until chilled through.

5. Garnish with chopped nuts, lemon zest and mixed spice, and serve chilled.

TIP:

This is a great gluten-free dessert!

Nutrient Analysis: PER SERVING: 146 cal (610kJ); Protein 2g; Total Fat 4g; Saturated Fat <1g; Carbohydrate 25g; Total Sugars 14g; Fiber 1g; Sodium 30mg; Potassium 143mg; Calcium 75mg

Complete Health Improvement Program – **EAT MORE** | 163

VARIATION: As an option, divide mixture using a tablespoon measure, roll into balls and coat with shredded coconut. Place in the freezer for 2 hours before serving.

Pecan and Raisin Slice

Preparation time: 10 minutes
Freeze time: 2 hours **Makes:** 23 slices

1 cup pecans
1½ cups raisins/sultanas
⅓ cup unsweetened shredded coconut, plus extra for coating
1 teaspoon mixed spice/pumpkin pie spice
1 teaspoon vanilla extract
1 tablespoon crystallized ginger, chopped
1½ teaspoons lime rind

1. Place all ingredients into a food processor and mix until well combined.

2. Roll mixture into a log with a diameter of 1 inch/2.5 centimeters, then cover with extra coconut. Roll in baking parchment and cover in foil to hold in place.

3. Place in freezer for 2 hours before serving. To serve, remove from freezer and slice into ½-inch/1½-centimeter slices, or as desired.

Nutrient Analysis: PER SLICE: 85 cal (358kJ); Protein 1g; Total Fat 5g; Saturated Fat 1g; Carbohydrate 9g; Total Sugars 9g; Fiber 1g; Sodium 5mg; Potassium 139mg; Calcium 10mg

Tropical Fruit Salad

Preparation time: 10 minutes
Cooking time: 2-5 minutes **Serves:** 8

2 cups fresh pineapple, diced
2½ cups fresh or frozen mango, diced
juice of 1 lime
¼ cup unsweetened shredded coconut
10 mint leaves, finely shredded

1. Preheat oven to 350°F/180°C. Place shredded coconut on an oven tray and toast in the oven for approximately 2 minutes or until golden brown.

2. Combine pineapple, mango, lime and mint together in a bowl.

3. Top with toasted coconut.

DID YOU KNOW? *Mangoes are high in fiber and can help improve digestion.*

Nutrient Analysis: PER SERVING: 66 cal (277kJ); Protein 1g; Total Fat 2g; Saturated Fat 1g; Carbohydrate 10g; Total Sugars 10g; Fiber 2g; Sodium 2mg; Potassium 201mg; Calcium 17mg

SERVING SUGGESTION: *Sprinkle with chia seeds and berries.*

VARIATION: Try making date and mixed nut balls—instead of adding 3 cups cashews, add 1 cup almonds, 1 cup pecans and 1 cup cashews.

GF ⏱ *Date, Cashew and Sesame Balls*

Preparation time: 10 minutes **Freeze time:** 2 hours **Makes:** 24

3 cups raw cashews
1 cup sesame seeds
3 cups pitted dates
1 tablespoon honey (optional)
½ teaspoon vanilla extract

1. Preheat oven to 400°F/200°C. Place cashews and sesame seeds on separate trays and roast for 8-10 minutes.

2. Place dates in a bowl and cover with boiling water. Leave to soak for 2-3 minutes. Drain dates and set aside to cool.

3. Blend roasted cashews in food processor or blender until medium chopped, remove and place in mixing bowl.

4. Place soaked dates, vanilla and honey into food processor, and mix until finely chopped.

5. Combine date mixture with cashews and mix well with hands.

6. Divide mixture using a tablespoon measure and roll into balls. Coat with roasted sesame seeds. Place in an airtight container and freeze for 2 hours before serving. Serve chilled.

Nutrient Analysis: PER BALL: 192 cal (802kJ); Protein 4g; Total Fat 12g; Saturated Fat 2g; Carbohydrate 15g; Total Sugars 13g; Fiber 3g; Sodium 5mg; Potassium 229mg; Calcium 17mg; Iron 1.6mg; Zinc 1.4mg

# Apple Pecan Cake

Preparation time: 20 minutes **Cooking time:** 35 minutes **Serves:** 12

½ cup chopped pecans
1 apple, unpeeled and diced
1 teaspoon cinnamon
⅔ cup non-dairy milk fortified with calcium/B12
⅓ cup pure maple syrup
1½ cups whole wheat flour
1 tablespoon baking powder
½ teaspoon salt (optional)
¾ cup apple sauce (unsweetened)
½ cup honey
1 tablespoon vanilla extract

1. Preheat oven to 350°F/175°C and lightly grease a 8-inch/20-centimeter round cake pan.

2. Sprinkle the pecans in the bottom of the cake pan, followed by the diced apple and cinnamon.

3. In a small bowl, combine ⅓ cup non-dairy milk with maple syrup. Pour over the pecans and apples.

4. In another bowl, stir together flour, baking powder, salt, apple sauce, honey, vanilla and remaining non-dairy milk to form a batter.

5. Spread this batter evenly over the pecans and apples.

6. Bake for 30 minutes or until a toothpick/skewer comes out clean.

7. Cool in pan, then hold serving plate on top of cake and flip over to serve.

Sugars are noted as being primarily sourced from refined sources, therefore should be consumed sparingly.

VARIATION:

Instead of making Apple Pecan Cake, make Apple Pecan Muffins. Evenly distribute batter in muffin tins for individual servings and reduce baking time to suit.

Nutrient Analysis: PER SERVING: 184 cal (769kJ); Protein 3g; Total Fat 4g; Saturated Fat <1g; Carbohydrate 33g; Total Sugars 21g; Fiber 3g; Sodium 346mg; Potassium 157mg; Calcium 33mg; Zinc 1.2mg

Recipe kindly provided by Fort Myers CHIP Chapter, Florida, USA.

NOTE: This dessert should only be consumed on special occasions. Choose small servings.

SERVING SUGGESTION: *Serve with walnuts, berries or Sweet Cashew Cream.*

Recipe kindly provided by London CHIP Chapter, Ontario, Canada.

 *Carrot Cake*

Preparation time: 20 minutes **Cooking time:** 35 minutes **Serves:** 12

1¼ **cups water**
1¼ **cups chopped dates**
1 **cup raisins/sultanas**
1 **teaspoon cinnamon**
1 **teaspoon ground ginger**
½ **teaspoon ground nutmeg**
2 **cups grated carrot**
½ **cup fresh orange juice**
2 **cups whole wheat flour**
1½ **teaspoons aluminium-free baking powder**
1½ **teaspoons baking soda**

1. Preheat oven to 350°F/180°C.

2. In a small saucepan, combine water, dates, raisins, cinnamon, ginger and nutmeg. Bring to a boil, reduce heat and simmer for 5 minutes.

3. Place the grated carrot in a large bowl. Pour the hot mixture over the top and allow to cool completely.

4. When carrot mixture is cool, add orange juice and stir well.

5. Add the dry ingredients to the wet ingredients and stir well to combine.

6. Pour mixture into a lightly oiled 9-inch/23-centimeter round cake tin. Bake for 30 minutes or until a toothpick/skewer comes out clean.

Majority of total sugars sourced from whole foods.

Nutrient Analysis: PER SERVING: 195 cal (817kJ); Protein 4g; Total Fat <1g; Saturated Fat <1g; Carbohydrate 41g; Total Sugars 25g; Fiber 6g; Sodium 366mg; Potassium 467mg; Calcium 55mg; Iron 1.9mg

TIP:

Why not freeze some for later? This is a great treat for when those unexpected visitors arrive.

Frozen Banana and Cherry Dessert Slice

Preparation time: 20-30 minutes **Freezing time:** Overnight **Serves:** 12

10 ripe frozen bananas
3 tablespoons lime juice
2 cups frozen or fresh pitted cherries

1. Chop 6 of the frozen bananas into chunks and allow to soften at room temperature for about 5 minutes.

2. Place chopped bananas and 2 tablespoons lime juice into food processor, and process on high until smooth and creamy. Place into a bowl and set aside in the freezer to prevent it from melting.

3. Repeat process with remaining 4 bananas and add remaining 1 tablespoon lime juice. When creamy, add cherries and continue processing until smooth.

4. Line a loaf tin with plastic wrap and alternate layers of banana and cherry mixtures until finished.

5. Return to freezer and allow to set for at least 3 hours (or preferably overnight).

6. When ready to serve, dip the base of the tin into hot water, then turn out onto a platter or board. Remove plastic wrap, slice and serve with Berry Sauce (see left).

Nutrient Analysis: PER SERVING: 106 cal (442kJ); Protein 2g; Total Fat <1g; Saturated Fat <1g; Carbohydrate 23g; Total Sugars 19g; Fiber 3g; Sodium 1mg; Potassium 391mg; Calcium 16mg

Berry Sauce

2 cups raspberries, blueberries or mixed berries
1 tablespoon honey
1 teaspoon lime juice
¼-½ cup water (as desired)

1. Place berries, honey, lime juice and water into a blender, and process on high until smooth.

SERVING SUGGESTION: *Serve with your choice of other fresh or frozen fruit.*

Raspberry Friands

Preparation time: 20 minutes **Cooking time:** 20 minutes **Serves:** 15

2 cups raw whole almonds
¼ cup whole wheat flour or gluten-free flour
¼ cup unsweetened shredded coconut
¼ teaspoon salt
1 teaspoon aluminium-free baking powder
⅔ cup apple sauce (unsweetened)
3 teaspoons vanilla extract
3 teaspoons lemon zest
½ cup oil
¼ cup honey
1 cup frozen raspberries
oil spray

1. Preheat oven to 325°C/160°C.

2. Grind almonds in blender or food processor by pulsing until they reach a meal-like texture. Pass through a sieve if mixture contains big lumps. Re-pulse big lumps only if present.

3. Mix all dry ingredients in a bowl.

4. Place apple sauce, vanilla, lemon zest, oil and honey in a separate bowl, and mix to combine.

5. Add the wet ingredients to the dry ingredients and mix together using a wooden spoon.

6. Gently fold in the raspberries.

7. Spray friand tin or muffin tin with oil. Fill tins and bake for 20 minutes or until golden on top.

DID YOU KNOW?

The fiber content of raspberries and blackberries is twice that of strawberries.

Do not over-grind the almonds or you will end up with almond butter.

Nutrient Analysis: PER SERVING: 238 cal (1037kJ); Protein 5g; Total Fat 18g; Saturated Fat 3g; Carbohydrate 16g; Total Sugars 10g; Fiber 4g; Sodium 109mg; Potassium 190mg; Calcium 7mg

Maple Cookies

Preparation time: 10 minutes **Cooking time:** 8-10 minutes **Makes:** 25 cookies

½ cup raw whole almonds
½ cup whole wheat flour
⅓ cup all-purpose flour
¼ cup maple syrup
¼ cup oil
1 teaspoon cinnamon
pecans for decoration

1. Preheat oven to 350°F/180°C.

2. Grind almonds in blender or food processor by pulsing until they reach a meal-like texture. Pass through a sieve if mixture contains big lumps. Re-pulse big lumps only if present.

3. Place almond meal, flour, maple syrup, oil and cinnamon in a bowl, and mix until well combined to form a firm dough.

4. Roll out dough 0.2 inches/0.5 centimeters thick and cut using a cookie cutter. Place on a baking sheet/tray lined with baking paper.

5. Place half a pecan on each and brush with extra maple syrup.

6. Bake in oven for 8 minutes or until golden brown.

DID YOU KNOW?

Choosing whole wheat flour over white flour will provide you with extra fiber.

Do not over-grind the almonds or you will end up with almond butter.

Nutrient Analysis: PER COOKIE: 85 cal (356kJ); Protein 1g; Total Fat 6g; Saturated Fat <1g; Carbohydrate 6g; Total Sugars 2g; Fiber 1g; Sodium 1mg; Potassium 53mg; Calcium 5mg

Conversion Table Guide

Use these tables as a guide to convert metric to imperial measurements. These tables are a rounded estimate, useful for cooking and are not an exact conversion of metric to imperial.

OVEN TEMPERATURES

Oven temperatures can vary depending on the type of oven you are using. It's always recommended to check the manufacturer's instructions first.

	Fahrenheit (°F)	Celsius (°C)
Very Slow	250	120
Slow	300	150
Warm	325	160
Moderate	350	180
Moderately hot	375-400	190-200
Hot	425	220
Very hot	450	230
Superhot	475+	250+

Source: National Measurement Institute: http://www.measurement. gov.au/Pages/MetricConversion.aspx Australian Government

NOTE: All recipes have been tested in Australian metric measurements.

LIQUID MEASUREMENTS :

AMERICAN CUP AND SPOON MEASUREMENTS

Spoons/Cups	Fluid Ounce *(fl oz)*	Milliliters *(ml)*
1 teaspoon	⅙ fl oz	5ml
1 tablespoon	½ fl oz	15ml
¼ cup	2 fl oz	56ml
⅓ cup	2.6 fl oz	75ml
½ cup	4 fl oz	112ml
1 cup	8 fl oz	225ml
2 cups	16 fl oz	450ml
4 cups	32 fl oz	900ml

METRIC CUP AND SPOON MEASURES

Spoons/Cups	Milliliters *(ml)*	Fluid Ounce *(fl oz)*
1 teaspoon	5ml	⅙ fl oz
1 tablespoon	20ml	½ fl oz
¼ cup	60ml	2 fl oz
⅓ cup	85ml	2 ⅔ fl oz
½ cup	125ml	4 fl oz
1 cup	250ml	8 fl oz
2 cups	500ml	16 fl oz
4 cups	1000ml/1 liter	32 fl oz

Measuring cups and spoons may vary slightly from one country to another, but the difference is generally not sufficient to affect a recipe.

DRY MEASURES

Imperial Ounces (oz) Pounds (lb)	Metric Grams (g) Kilograms (kg)
⅓ oz	10g
½ oz	15g
1 oz	30g
2 oz	60g
3 oz	85g
4 oz	115g
5 oz	140g
6 oz	170g
7 oz	200g
8 oz	230g
9 oz	255g
10 oz	285g
11 oz	310g
12 oz	340g
13 oz	370g
14 oz	400g
15 oz	425g
16 oz/1 lb	450g
32 oz/2 lb	900g

Recipe Index

A

Almond Cranberry
Cookies, 159

Apple and Rhubarb
with Oat Clusters, 40

Apple Pecan Cake, 168

Arugula, Eggplant
and Bean Salad, 86

Avocado and Cashew
Cream Parfait, 160

B

Beet and Bean Dip, 150

Beet and Blueberry
Blitz, 44

Berry Oat Smoothie, 44

Black Bean
and Avocado Salad, 73

Black Bean Stew, 124

Brown Rice, 37

Butternut
Squash Tagine, 47

C

Cabbage and
Pineapple Salad, 81

Carrot Cake, 171

Cashew Cheese, 153

Cashew Cheese
and Salad Pita Pocket, 109

Chunky Roast Tomato
Pasta Salad, 52

Corn Bread, 125

Corn and Pea Fritters, 113

Cornmeal/Polenta, 37

Cornmeal Cake
with Citrus Zest, 163

Cracked Wheat, 36

Creamy Cashew
White Sauce, 146

Creamy Mushrooms, 66

Cucumber
and Dill Salad, 77

D

Date, Apricot
and Ginger Jam, 149

Date, Cashew
and Sesame Balls, 167

E

Eggless Mayonnaise, 146

F

Fennel Citrus Salad, 43

Frozen Banana and
Cherry Dessert Slice, 172

G

Garbanzo and
Eggplant Stew, 127

Garden Rice Salad, 74

Green Pea and
Cilantro Soup, 102

H

Homemade Baked
Beans, 55

Honey and Ginger
Carrots, 90

Hummus Dip, 152

Hummus and Tabbouleh
Wrap, 106

K

Kale and Banana
Boost, 44

Kale and Beet Salad, 70

Kale with Pine Nuts, 90

L

Lentil and Sesame
Rissoles, 120

Lentil and Vegetable
Hotpot, 56

Lentil Shepherd's Pie, 128

M

Maple Cookies, 176

Minestrone Soup, 51

Minted Pea Hummus, 150

Mushroom and
Lentil Stew, 123

N

Nutty Potato Bites, 136

O

Oat and Cashew Waffles, 63

P

Pearl Barley, 39

Pecan and Raisin Slice, 164

Pesto, 52

Potato and Corn
Chowder, 97

Potato and Corn
Salad, 75

Potato Rosti, 65

Pumpkin and
Garbanzo Satay, 131

Pumpkin and Spice Pie, 156

Pumpkin and Spinach
Lasagna, 142

Pumpkin Risotto Bites, 140

Q

Quick Bircher Muesli
with Chia, 62

Quick Pizza Crust, 117

Quinoa, 39

Quinoa and Fig Salad with Lemon Dressing, 82

R
Raspberry Friands, 175

Red Lentil and Vegetable Dahl, 135

Red Pepper and Lima Bean Dip, 150

Roast Pepper and Pumpkin Soup, 98

Roast Vegetable Quiche, 132

Roast Vegetable and Lentil Lasagna, 138

Rolled Oats, 36

S
Salsa Salad, 42

Savory Cashew Cream, 146

Scrambled Tofu and Salad Wrap, 110

Split Pea and Cumin Hotpot, 48

Steamed Vegetables with Creamy Cashew White Sauce, 93

Strawberry Spinach Salad, 85

Sweet Cashew Cream, 149

Sweet Potatoes with Orange Sauce, 89

T
Tomato and Basil Sauce, 147

Tortilla Cups with Beans and Salad, 114

Tropical Fruit Salad, 165

W
Warm Roast Vegetable Salad, 78

White Bean and Sweet Potato Soup with Greens, 101

Wholesome Banana Pancakes, 60

Complete Health Improvement Program – **EAT MORE** | 181

Notes

Notes

Notes